The No-Fuss

BREAD MACHINE
COOKBOOK

For general information on our other products and services or to obtain technical support, please contact our Customer Care Department within the US at (866) 744-2665, or outside the US at (510) 253-0500.

Rockridge Press publishes its books in a variety of electronic and print formats. Some content that appears in print may not be available in electronic books, and vice versa.

Trademarks: Rockridge Press and the Rockridge Press logo are trademarks or registered trademarks of Callisto Media Inc. and/or its affiliates, in the United States and other countries, and may not be used without written permission. All other trademarks are the property of their respective owners. Rockridge Press is not associated with any product or vendor mentioned in this book.

Photography © 2016 by Shannon Douglas

ISBN: Print 978-1-62315-753-1 | eBook 978-1-62315-754-8

The No-Fuss
BREAD MACHINE
COOKBOOK

*Hands-Off Recipes for
Perfect Homemade Bread*

Michelle Anderson

ROCKRIDGE
PRESS

CONTENTS

INTRODUCTION

Making bread is an almost primal activity, with the very physical kneading, careful supervision of the rising dough, and the deep satisfaction of serving piping hot bread to your family. It is also incredible that a few simple ingredients can produce such a wonderfully complex finished food. Bread is a delight and can seem like culinary magic. Yet, bread making is a skill that even many professional chefs do not master because it takes time (and well-developed biceps) to create loaves for service and to offer to clients. In most cases, you have to start at 3:00 a.m. to allow for the completion of all the bread-making steps, and many people do not have this sort of commitment or patience.

Outside of professional kitchens, most people in today's fast-paced world do not have time to make homemade bread, especially when many different types of bread can be purchased at almost every store. Yet, commercially made loaves are pale, insignificant versions of the rich, delicious bread you can create yourself with a handy bread machine. Even someone with the most hectic schedule in the world has 5 minutes to load a bread machine and set a timer to produce hot, fragrant bread that is ready to eat when you come through the door at the end of the day. Cutting the first slice of a new loaf—usually while it is too warm—never loses its magic, and the first bite is always sublime.

This book will give you a basic understanding of how ingredients combine to produce bread and which factors can create less-than-perfect results. You will be introduced to a collection of recipes that can be used, for the most part, in 1-pound, 1½-pound, and 2-pound bread machines. These recipes can serve as your foundation for new bread experiences and allow you to experience all the fun of serving homemade bread to friends and family.

—Chapter One—
BAKING MADE EASY

Bread machines are undeniably convenient, and the bread that comes out of them is just as delicious—if not more so—than loaves you might find in a high-end bakery. Does bread machine bread look as gorgeously formed? No, but if you can get past the signature square edges and understand the visual result might not be perfect, you will probably never buy commercially made bread again. Even loaves that turn out slightly misshapen or rise a little too high will taste phenomenal dipped into soup or spread with a little sweet butter.

If you love bread in all its variations, from crusty French bread to moist banana quick bread, and you are willing to create bread without hands-on work, this book will be perfect for you. Discover new favorite recipes or adapt the recipes you already use with your own bread machine. Dive in and start baking!

Why We Love Bread Machines

The main reason you will love your bread machine is the incredible variety of loaves you can create and enjoy without spending hours in the kitchen. There is something satisfying about popping out fragrant, fresh bread from the bucket knowing you made it yourself. However, here are some other reasons your bread machine will quickly become your favorite kitchen appliance:

- **Saves power.** Think about how warm your kitchen gets when you bake anything in the oven, especially during the summer months. Escaping heat is money out of your pocket, and even if you have a very well-insulated oven, it still costs more to run an oven than a bread machine. The power usage of a standard bread machine is thought to be about the same as or less than a coffeemaker, about 9 kilowatt-hours for 15 hours a month.

- **Set it and forget it.** You have time to do other tasks, run errands, or make the rest of a big meal without supervising the bread in the machine. Traditional bread making is more hands-on and requires a significant amount of time.

- **Cleanup is a breeze.** If you have ever made bread without a machine, you will be familiar with the dirty bowls, flour mess from kneading the dough, and washing up the pans or baking sheets. With the bread machine, you just dump the ingredients in and wash a couple measuring cups and spoons. Plus, bread machine buckets wipe off easily after the loaf is out.

- **Control over ingredients.** Knowing exactly what is in the food you set on the table is reassuring, especially if you have someone in the family with allergies or food issues. The ingredients you buy are completely under your control, so there are no unrecognizable ingredients in the finished loaf.

- **Saves money.** Almost all the ingredients you put into bread can be bought in bulk, which is the best way to save money.

The Glory of Gluten

Gluten is a protein composite found in cereal grains that produces the texture and structure of baked goods. Gluten is made up of two protein groups, gliadin and glutenin, which bind together when mixed with water. The gliadin is responsible for gluten's ability to be stretched, and glutenin contributes to gluten's ability to return to its initial position after stretching. As the dough is mixed, a network of gluten strands is formed. The longer this process goes on, the stronger these strands become. This gluten network traps the gases produced by yeast and allows the bread to rise. Some of the factors that affect gluten development include:

- **Type of flour.** The protein content and quality of bread will vary depending on the type of flour.

- **Amount of water.** Gluten doesn't exist without water.

- **Fat.** Fat coats the proteins, blocking hydration and the formation of long gluten strands.

- **Salt.** Salt makes gluten stronger and stickier.

- **Sugar.** Sugar attaches to the water molecules before they can bind the protein groups together.

Bread Machine Techniques

The processes that occur in a bread machine are not that different than those you use when making bread by hand. They are just less work and mess. The primary techniques used in making bread from a bread machine are:

- **Mixing and resting.** The ingredients are mixed together well and then allowed to rest before kneading.

- **Kneading.** This technique creates long strands of gluten. Kneading squishes, stretches, turns, and presses the dough for 20 to 30 minutes, depending on the machine and setting.

THE ONLY INGREDIENTS YOU NEED

The ingredients needed for bread making are very simple: flour, yeast, salt, and liquid. There are other ingredients that add flavor, texture, and nutrition to your bread, such as sugar, fats, and eggs. The basic ingredients include:

Flour is the foundation of bread. The protein and gluten in flour forms a network that traps the carbon dioxide and alcohol produced by the yeast. Flour also provides simple sugar to feed the yeast and it provides flavor, depending on the type of flour used in the recipe.

Yeast is a living organism that multiplies when the right amount of moisture, food, and heat are applied. Rapidly multiplying yeast gives off carbon dioxide and ethyl alcohol. When yeast is allowed to go through its life cycle completely, the finished bread is more flavorful. The best yeast for bread machines is bread machine yeast or active dry yeast, depending on your bread machine model.

Salt strengthens gluten and slows the rise of the bread by retarding the action of the yeast. A slower rise allows the flavors of the bread to develop better, and it will be less likely the bread will rise too much.

Liquid activates the yeast and dissolves the other ingredients. The most commonly used liquid is water, but ingredients such as milk can also be substituted. Bread made with water will have a crisper crust, but milk produces rich, tender bread that offers more nutrition and browns easier.

Oils and fats add flavor, create a tender texture, and help brown the crust. Bread made with fat stays fresh longer because moisture loss in the bread is slowed. This component can also inhibit gluten formation, so the bread does not rise as high.

Sugar is the source of food for the yeast. It also adds sweetness, tenderness, and color to the crust. Too much sugar can inhibit gluten growth or cause the dough to rise too much and collapse. Other sweeteners can replace sugar, such as honey, molasses, maple syrup, brown sugar, and corn syrup.

Eggs add protein, flavor, color, and a tender crust. Eggs contain an emulsifier, lecithin, which helps create a consistent texture, and a leavening agent, which helps the bread rise well.

- **First rise.** This is also called bulk fermentation. Yeast converts the sugar into alcohol, which provides flavor, and carbon dioxide, which provides structure as it inflates the gluten framework.

- **Stir down (1 and 2).** The paddles rotate to bring the loaf down and redistribute the dough before the second and third rise.

- **Second and third rise.** The second rise is about 15 minutes. At the end of the third rise, the loaf will almost double in size.

- **Baking.** There will be one final growth spurt for the yeast in the dough in the first 5 minutes or so of the baking process, and the bread bakes into the finished loaf. Baking time and temperature will depend on the size, type, and crust setting of the loaf.

Cycles and Settings

The idea of choosing a bread machine can be overwhelming, but most machines have a similar assortment of programmed cycles with precise times and temperatures, so different breads turn out perfectly—or close to perfect. There might be some variation, but the usual cycles are:

- **Basic/White.** This is a default setting for yeast breads that use white flour and a bit of whole-wheat or oat flour. This cycle is versatile and the browning is perfect.

- **Quick/Rapid.** This setting is for recipes specifying that bread can be made in less time. The rise times are shortened or there is only one rise.

- **Sweet.** The lower baking temperatures of this setting are for yeast breads that have more sugar, honey, or dried fruit.

- **Whole-Wheat/Whole-Grain.** The rise time on whole-wheat or whole-grain breads is longer than in the Basic cycle for white bread because the gluten needs more time to work.

- **French.** This is a longer cycle designed to create a gorgeous, hard crust such as the crust on European-style breads.

- **Quick Bread.** Quick breads do not contain yeast and do not need time to rise, so this cycle is usually only 2 hours.

- **Jam.** This handy cycle makes jam using very hot temperatures, so be careful when removing the bread pan.

- **Dough.** If you love making all types of bread but hate the work that goes into kneading and mixing, this setting is a must. The dough is then cooked in a conventional oven.

- **Gluten-Free.** Flours that contain no gluten can be very tricky to bake. This setting still has a rise time, but it is not as long as the other cycles.

- **Other/Custom.** This might include the option to extend baking or rise times by increments, preset baking times, or some other function that is explained in your manual.

High Altitude

Any place with an elevation of 3,000 feet or higher is considered to be a high-altitude area. In these areas, the atmosphere is drier and air pressure is lower, creating two basic issues with bread: the dough is drier and it rises faster. These factors create a challenge, but there are strategies you can employ to ensure wonderful results. Try implementing the tips one at a time until you come up with a winning combination for the altitude where you live.

- **Use a bread machine with customizable programs.** This way, you can adjust the cycles to suit your needs.

- **Make smaller loaves.** Smaller loaves require less proofing time and reduce overproofing.

- **Increase the moisture.** Use 2 to 4 tablespoons of liquid per cup of flour.

- **Use colder ingredients**. For example, use liquids straight from the refrigerator.

- **Increase the salt.** Try increasing the salt in your recipes by ⅛ to ¼ teaspoon.

- **Decrease the yeast.** Try decreasing the yeast in your recipes by ⅛ to ½ teaspoon.
- **Decrease the sugar.** Try decreasing the sugar or sweeteners in your recipe by 1 to 2 teaspoons.

Storing Your Bread

Bread machine bread is so delicious, you might create more than you, your family, and your friends can eat in one sitting. Here are some tips for storing your bread machine creations:

Dough. After the kneading cycle, remove the dough from the machine. If you plan on using the dough within three days, you can store it in the refrigerator. Form the dough into a disk and place it in a sealable freezer bag, or store the dough in a lightly oiled bowl covered with plastic wrap. Yeast action will not stop in the refrigerator, so punch the dough down until it is completely chilled, and then once a day. When you are ready to bake bread, remove the dough from the refrigerator, shape it, let it rise, and bake. Bread machine dough has no preservatives, so freeze it if you aren't baking it in three days. Form the dough into a disk and place it in a sealable freezer bag. You can freeze bread dough for up to a month. When you are ready to bake the bread, remove the dough from the freezer, store it in the refrigerator overnight, shape it, let it rise, and bake. You can shape the dough into braids, loaves, knots, or other shapes before refrigerating or freezing it. Wrap the shapes tightly and store in the refrigerator (if you are baking within 24 hours) or the freezer. At the right time, unwrap the dough, allow it to rise at room temperature, and bake it.

Baked Bread. Once your baked bread is cooled, wrap the loaf in plastic wrap or a freezer bag and place it in the refrigerator or freezer. You can freeze baked bread for up to 6 months. To thaw the bread, remove it from the freezer, unwrap the loaf partially, and let it sit at room temperature. If you want to serve warm bread after refrigerating or freezing a loaf, wrap the bread in aluminum foil, and bake it in an oven preheated to 300°F for 10 to 15 minutes.

About the Recipes

Most of the recipes that follow have three variations, which take into account the size of bread machine you are using. An exception is the quick breads, which are not specialized. Quick breads have no rise times and can be made in most bread machines with a few tweaks on baking time, if necessary.

Anytime a recipe calls for butter, I baked it using salted butter, but you can use unsalted butter if you like. Anytime a recipe calls for milk, I baked it using 2 percent milk, but you can achieve similar results with any kind of milk. If you want to use a timer for your bread and the recipe calls for milk as the primary liquid, you can substitute water for milk without much change in the bread.

Often I'll ask you to add ingredients in the order recommended by your bread machine's manufacturer. All bread machines are different; some ask you to add wet ingredients first, while others start with dry. Consult the manual for your particular bread machine ahead of time.

Anytime I ask you to bring an ingredient to a specific temperature before adding it to your recipe, please take my word for it! These recipes won't work if you simply use all ingredients at room temperature. You'll need a thermometer to measure the temperature of these ingredients beforehand.

Keep in mind that many variables will affect the finished loaf, such as the kind of flour used (protein content), type of yeast, temperature of ingredients, and your measuring tools. Sometimes your bread will be so perfect, you want to post a picture of it. The next time you make the same recipe, a cooler kitchen temperature does not allow a good rise. Don't despair! Even an imperfect-looking loaf of bread can be delicious.

TROUBLESHOOTING

Your success making bread in a bread machine can be affected by many different factors, which means a recipe that turns out a wonderful loaf one day may not produce the same loaf a week later. The bread will probably still be delicious, but it might not look exactly right. Here are some common bread-making issues:

No rise

- Yeast is old or stored improperly

- Measurement of ingredients is wrong

- Flour has low gluten content

- Too little yeast

- Temperature of ingredients is too high

- Temperature of ingredients is too low

- Too much salt

- Too much or too little sugar

- Salt came in contact with the yeast

Too much rise

- Too much yeast

- Too little salt

- Water temperature is incorrect

- Bucket is too small for the recipe size

Dense and short

- Bread doesn't rise (see No rise)

- Ingredients were added in the wrong order

- Dough is too dry; there is too much flour (not enough liquid)

- Size of the bucket is too large for the recipe

- Too much whole-grain flour or whole grains

- Too much dried fruit

- Too many other ingredients such as vegetables, nuts, or coconut

Crust too thick

- Bread is left in the machine after the baking cycle is complete

- Flour has too little gluten

- Bread doesn't rise high enough (see No rise)

Crust too dark

- Crust setting is too dark

- Bread is left in the machine after the baking cycle is complete

- Too much sugar

$\longrightarrow$

Crust too light

- Crust setting is too light

- Too little sugar

- Recipe size is too large for the bucket

Mushroom top

- Too much yeast

- Too much water

- Ingredients are out of proportion or measured wrong

- Too much sugar or too many sweet ingredients

- Size of the bucket is too small for the recipe

Sunken top

- Bread machine was opened during baking cycle

- Humid or warm weather

- Too much liquid in the recipe

- Liquid ingredients are too warm

- Ingredients were measured wrong or out of proportion

- Bread rose too far, disrupting the baking and cooling cycles

- Too much yeast

Coarse texture

- Too much liquid

- Too little salt

- Too much yeast

- Fruit or vegetables too moist

- Weather too warm or humid

Gummy

- Too much sugar

- Too much liquid or too many wet ingredients

- Temperature outside the machine is too cold

- Thermostat in the machine is defective

—Chapter Two—

BASIC BREADS

Everyday White Bread

PREP TIME IS 10 MINUTES OR LESS

If you are partial to a tender, fine-textured white bread that is perfect for toast, sandwiches, and bread pudding recipes, look no further than this golden beauty. If you like a darker crust on your bread, try the medium setting first because it will probably create the shade of crust you desire. The inside will stay tender no matter what crust setting you use for the loaf.

8 SLICES / 1 POUND	12 SLICES / 1½ POUNDS	16 SLICES / 2 POUNDS
¾ cup water, at 80°F to 90°F	1⅛ cups water, at 80°F to 90°F	1½ cups water, at 80°F to 90°F
1 tablespoon melted butter, cooled	1½ tablespoons melted butter, cooled	2 tablespoons melted butter, cooled
1 tablespoon sugar	1½ tablespoons sugar	2 tablespoons sugar
¾ teaspoon salt	1 teaspoon salt	2 teaspoons salt
2 tablespoons skim milk powder	3 tablespoons skim milk powder	¼ cup skim milk powder
2 cups white bread flour	3 cups white bread flour	4 cups white bread flour
¾ teaspoon bread machine or instant yeast	1¼ teaspoons bread machine or instant yeast	1½ teaspoons bread machine or instant yeast

1. Place the ingredients in your bread machine as recommended by the manufacturer.
2. Program the machine for Basic/White bread, select light or medium crust, and press Start.
3. When the loaf is done, remove the bucket from the machine.
4. Let the loaf cool for 5 minutes.
5. Gently shake the bucket to remove the loaf, and turn it out onto a rack to cool.

"Did You Know?" Powdered milk is usually made from skim milk. This is because the fat particles in regular milk could go rancid, shortening the shelf life of powdered milk, despite the fact that all the water has been removed. Whenever possible, smell the powdered milk, and if there is any odor at all, do not buy it.

PER SERVING (1 SLICE): CALORIES: 140; TOTAL FAT: 2G; SATURATED FAT: 1G; CARBOHYDRATES: 27G; FIBER: 1G; SODIUM: 215MG; PROTEIN: 4G

Honey Whole-Wheat Bread

PREP TIME IS 10 MINUTES OR LESS

Whole-wheat bread is a healthy choice when it comes to bread options. You will be thrilled when you create a loaf of fiber-rich goodness that has only five ingredients beyond the water and yeast. The honey contributes just a hint of sweetness, and added white bread flour ensures a firm but airy texture.

8 SLICES / 1 POUND	12 SLICES / 1 ½ POUNDS	16 SLICES / 2 POUNDS
¾ cup water, at 80°F to 90°F	1 ⅛ cups water, at 80°F to 90°F	1 ½ cups water, at 80°F to 90°F
1 tablespoon honey	2 tablespoons honey	3 tablespoons honey
1 tablespoon melted butter, cooled	1 ½ tablespoons melted butter, cooled	2 tablespoons melted butter, cooled
½ teaspoon salt	¾ teaspoon salt	1 teaspoon salt
2 cups whole-wheat flour	2 ½ cups whole-wheat flour	3 ¼ cups whole-wheat flour
½ cup white bread flour	¾ cup white bread flour	1 cup white bread flour
1 teaspoon bread machine or instant yeast	1 ½ teaspoons bread machine or instant yeast	2 teaspoons bread machine or instant yeast

1. Place the ingredients in your bread machine as recommended by the manufacturer.
2. Program the machine for Basic/White bread, select light or medium crust, and press Start.
3. When the loaf is done, remove the bucket from the machine.
4. Let the loaf cool for 5 minutes.
5. Gently shake the bucket to remove the loaf, and turn it out onto a rack to cool.

Ingredient tip: The taste of honey changes depending on what flowers provide the nectar collected by the bees. Try different types of honey, such as robust buckwheat honey or flowery, pale alfalfa honey, to see how the taste of the bread is affected.

PER SERVING (1 SLICE): CALORIES: 148; TOTAL FAT: 2G; SATURATED FAT: 1G; CARBOHYDRATES: 29G; FIBER: 1G; SODIUM: 159MG; PROTEIN: 4G

Molasses Wheat Bread

PREP TIME IS 10 MINUTES OR LESS

Be prepared for your family to request this tantalizing bread again and again every time you get out your bread machine. The sweetness of a generous amount of honey and a bit of sugar is tempered by the rich and slight bitter taste of molasses. The molasses and cocoa create a glorious dark brown bread, which is fabulous piled with smoked turkey and creamy Swiss cheese.

8 SLICES / 1 POUND	12 SLICES / 1½ POUNDS	16 SLICES / 2 POUNDS
½ cup water, at 80°F to 90°F	¾ cup water, at 80°F to 90°F	1 cup water, at 80°F to 90°F
¼ cup milk, at 80°F	⅓ cup milk, at 80°F	½ cup milk, at 80°F
2 teaspoons melted butter, cooled	1 tablespoon melted butter, cooled	2 tablespoons melted butter, cooled
2 tablespoons honey	3¾ tablespoons honey	5 tablespoons honey
1 tablespoon molasses	2 tablespoons molasses	3 tablespoons molasses
1 teaspoon sugar	2 teaspoons sugar	1 tablespoon sugar
1 tablespoon skim milk powder	2 tablespoons skim milk powder	3 tablespoons skim milk powder
½ teaspoon salt	¾ teaspoon salt	1 teaspoon salt
1 teaspoon unsweetened cocoa powder	2 teaspoons unsweetened cocoa powder	1 tablespoon unsweetened cocoa powder
1¼ cups whole-wheat flour	1¾ cups whole-wheat flour	2½ cups whole-wheat flour
1 cup white bread flour	1¼ cups white bread flour	2 cups white bread flour
1 teaspoon bread machine yeast or instant yeast	1⅛ teaspoons bread machine yeast or instant yeast	1½ teaspoons bread machine or instant yeast

1. Place the ingredients in your bread machine as recommended by the manufacturer.

2. Program the machine for Basic/White bread, select light or medium crust, and press Start.

3. When the loaf is done, remove the bucket from the machine.

4. Let the loaf cool for 5 minutes.

5. Gently shake the bucket to remove the loaf, and turn it out onto a rack to cool.

Ingredient tip: Look for unsulphured molasses because it is sweeter and lacks the slight chemical taste of sulphured products. Also, this bread is best with sticky, rich dark or blackstrap molasses instead of light-colored molasses.

PER SERVING (1 SLICE): CALORIES: 164; TOTAL FAT: 2G; SATURATED FAT: 1G; CARBOHYDRATES: 34G; FIBER: 1G; SODIUM: 166MG; PROTEIN: 4G

100 Percent Whole-Wheat Bread

PREP TIME IS 10 MINUTES OR LESS

Most commercial breads stating they are 100 percent whole-wheat use a certain percentage of white flour for structure so the bread rises easily and isn't as dense. The whole-wheat flour in this recipe is a bread flour rather than plain whole-wheat flour, so it is designed to rise with added wheat gluten right in the flour. If you are using regular whole-wheat flour, you might want to consider adding wheat gluten so the bread isn't as heavy.

8 SLICES / 1 POUND	12 SLICES / 1½ POUNDS	16 SLICES / 2 POUNDS
¾ cup water, at 80°F to 90°F	1⅛ cups water, at 80°F to 90°F	1½ cups water, at 80°F to 90°F
1½ tablespoons melted butter, cooled	2¼ tablespoons melted butter, cooled	3 tablespoons melted butter, cooled
1½ tablespoons honey	2¼ tablespoons honey	3 tablespoons honey
¾ teaspoon salt	1⅛ teaspoons salt	1½ teaspoons salt
2 cups whole-wheat bread flour	3 cups whole-wheat bread flour	3¾ cups whole-wheat bread flour
1 teaspoon bread machine or instant yeast	1½ teaspoons bread machine or instant yeast	2 teaspoons bread machine or instant yeast

1. Place the ingredients in your bread machine as recommended by the manufacturer.
2. Program the machine for Whole-Wheat/Whole-Grain bread, select light or medium crust, and press Start.
3. When the loaf is done, remove the bucket from the machine.
4. Let the loaf cool for 5 minutes.
5. Gently shake the bucket to remove the loaf, and turn it out onto a rack to cool.

"Did You Know?" Whole-wheat flour contains the entire wheat berry—endosperm, bran, and germ—unlike white flour, which is made up of only the endosperm. This means whole-wheat flour is extremely nutritious and packed with healthy fiber, vitamins, and minerals.

PER SERVING (1 SLICE): CALORIES: 146; TOTAL FAT: 3G; SATURATED FAT: 1G; CARBOHYDRATES: 27G; FIBER: 1G; SODIUM: 210MG; PROTEIN: 3G

Crusty French Bread

PREP TIME IS 10 MINUTES OR LESS

Many French bread recipes that start in a bread machine do not end there; the dough is taken out, formed into loaves, allowed to rise, and baked in a conventional oven. With this recipe, you can make spectacular golden French bread from start to finish in the machine. Your family will be delighted to eat fresh crusty bread with a steaming bowl of spaghetti and meatballs for Sunday dinner.

8 SLICES / 1 POUND	12 SLICES / 1½ POUNDS	16 SLICES / 2 POUNDS
⅔ cup water, at 80°F to 90°F	1 cup water, at 80°F to 90°F	1¼ cups water, at 80°F to 90°F
2 teaspoons olive oil	1¼ tablespoons olive oil	1½ tablespoons olive oil
1 tablespoon sugar	2 tablespoons sugar	2 tablespoons sugar
⅔ teaspoon salt	1¼ teaspoons salt	1½ teaspoons salt
2 cups white bread flour	3 cups white bread flour	4 cups white bread flour
1 teaspoon bread machine or instant yeast	1¼ teaspoons bread machine or instant yeast	1½ teaspoons bread machine or instant yeast

1. Place the ingredients in your bread machine as recommended by the manufacturer.
2. Program the machine for French bread, select light or medium crust, and press Start.
3. When the loaf is done, remove the bucket from the machine.
4. Let the loaf cool for 5 minutes.
5. Gently shake the bucket to remove the loaf, and turn it out onto a rack to cool.

Machine tip: If you do not have a French bread setting on your bread machine, use the Basic/White setting and select medium crust.

PER SERVING (1 SLICE): CALORIES: 135; TOTAL FAT: 2G; SATURATED FAT: 0G; CARBOHYDRATES: 26G; FIBER: 1G; SODIUM: 245MG; PROTEIN: 3G

Pumpernickel Bread

PREP TIME IS 10 MINUTES OR LESS

Traditional pumpernickel bread is baked entirely with rye flour, which made this German creation very dense and heavy. The addition of whole-wheat flour and white flour lightens the texture without taking away any of the rich flavor. This bread was traditionally baked in a steam oven for up to 20 hours to create the signature dark color, but the same color is created using cocoa and molasses in most modern recipes.

8 SLICES / 1 POUND	12 SLICES / 1 ½ POUNDS	16 SLICES / 2 POUNDS
½ cup water, at 80°F to 90°F	¾ cup water, at 80°F to 90°F	1 cup water, at 80°F to 90°F
¼ cup brewed coffee, at 80°F to 90°F	⅓ cup brewed coffee, at 80°F to 90°F	½ cup brewed coffee, at 80°F to 90°F
2 tablespoons dark molasses	3 tablespoons dark molasses	¼ cup dark molasses
5 teaspoons sugar	2 ½ tablespoons sugar	2 tablespoons sugar
4 teaspoons melted butter, cooled	2 tablespoons melted butter, cooled	4 teaspoons melted butter, cooled
1 tablespoon powdered skim milk	1 ½ tablespoons powdered skim milk	1 tablespoon powdered skim milk
1 teaspoon salt	1 ½ teaspoons salt	1 teaspoon salt
4 teaspoons unsweetened cocoa powder	2 tablespoons unsweetened cocoa powder	2 tablespoons unsweetened cocoa powder
⅔ cup dark rye flour	1 cup dark rye flour	1 ⅓ cups dark rye flour
½ cup whole-wheat bread flour	¾ cup whole-wheat bread flour	1 cup whole-wheat bread flour
1 teaspoon caraway seeds	2 teaspoons caraway seeds	1 tablespoon caraway seeds
1 cup white bread flour	1 ½ cups white bread flour	2 cups white bread flour
1 ½ teaspoons bread machine or active dry yeast	2 ¼ teaspoons bread machine or active dry yeast	2 ¼ teaspoons bread machine or active dry yeast

1. Place the ingredients in your bread machine as recommended by the manufacturer.

2. Program the machine for Basic/White bread, select light or medium crust, and press Start.

3. When the loaf is done, remove the bucket from the machine.

4. Let the loaf cool for 5 minutes.

5. Gently shake the bucket to remove the loaf, and turn it out onto a rack to cool.

Cooking tip: Rye flour has a very low gluten count, so it does not create fluffy, high-rising loaves of bread. The dough created for rye bread tends to look stickier than other dough, but resist the impulse to add more flour because this will create a tough loaf.

PER SERVING (1 SLICE): CALORIES: 168; TOTAL FAT: 3G; SATURATED FAT: 1G; CARBOHYDRATES: 33G; FIBER: 4G; SODIUM: 311MG; PROTEIN: 5G

Lovely Oatmeal Bread

PREP TIME IS 10 MINUTES OR LESS

Simple morning toast becomes a treat when you pop a couple slices of this rich, tender bread in your toaster. The bread cuts easily without buckling or crumbling, especially if you store it sealed in a freezer bag to retain moisture. Try it with almond butter and honey as a delectable fiber-packed start to the day.

8 SLICES / 1 POUND	12 SLICES / 1½ POUNDS	16 SLICES / 2 POUNDS
¾ cup water, at 80°F to 90°F	1⅛ cups water, at 80°F to 90°F	1½ cups water, at 80°F to 90°F
2 tablespoons melted butter, cooled	3 tablespoons melted butter, cooled	¼ cup melted butter, cooled
2 tablespoons sugar	3 tablespoons sugar	¼ cup sugar
1 teaspoon salt	1½ teaspoons salt	2 teaspoons salt
¾ cup quick oats	1 cup quick oats	1½ cups quick oats
1½ cups white bread flour	2¼ cups white bread flour	3 cups white bread flour
1 teaspoon bread machine or instant yeast	1½ teaspoons bread machine or instant yeast	2 teaspoons bread machine or instant yeast

1. Place the ingredients in your bread machine as recommended by the manufacturer.
2. Program the machine for Basic/White bread, select light or medium crust, and press Start.
3. When the loaf is done, remove the bucket from the machine.
4. Let the loaf cool for 5 minutes.
5. Gently shake the bucket to remove the loaf, and turn it out onto a rack to cool.

Ingredient tip: Do not substitute large flake oats for the quick oats in this recipe or the texture will be wrong in your finished bread. Quick oats are chopped up so they absorb liquids easier and cook faster.

PER SERVING (1 SLICE): CALORIES: 149; TOTAL FAT: 4G; SATURATED FAT: 2G; CARBOHYDRATES: 26G; FIBER: 1G; SODIUM: 312MG; PROTEIN: 4G

Oat Bran Molasses Bread

PREP TIME IS 10 MINUTES OR LESS

Oat bran is completely different from rolled oats or whole flake oats, so make sure you pick up the correct product at your local grocery store. Oat bran is the husk that is removed from the oat grain, and it is extremely high in fiber. You might find this bread does not rise quite as high because the edges of the bran are sharp, and they cut the rising gluten.

8 SLICES / 1 POUND	12 SLICES / 1½ POUNDS	16 SLICES / 2 POUNDS
½ cup water, at 80°F to 90°F	¾ cup water, at 80°F to 90°F	1 cup water, at 80°F to 90°F
1½ tablespoons melted butter, cooled	2¼ tablespoons melted butter, cooled	3 tablespoons melted butter, cooled
2 tablespoons blackstrap molasses	3 tablespoons blackstrap molasses	¼ cup blackstrap molasses
¼ teaspoon salt	⅓ teaspoon salt	½ teaspoon salt
⅛ teaspoon ground nutmeg	¼ teaspoon ground nutmeg	¼ teaspoon ground nutmeg
½ cup oat bran	¾ cup oat bran	1 cup oat bran
1½ cups whole-wheat bread flour	2¼ cups whole-wheat bread flour	3 cups whole-wheat bread flour
1⅛ teaspoons bread machine or instant yeast	1⅔ teaspoons bread machine or instant yeast	2¼ teaspoons bread machine or instant yeast

1. Place the ingredients in your bread machine as recommended by the manufacturer.
2. Program the machine for Whole-Wheat/Whole-Grain bread, select light or medium crust, and press Start.
3. When the loaf is done, remove the bucket from the machine.
4. Let the loaf cool for 5 minutes.
5. Gently shake the bucket to remove the loaf, and turn it out onto a rack to cool.

Decoration tip: Lightly brush the warm loaf with melted butter when you pop it out of the bucket, and scatter toasted whole oats on the top. The butter will create a lovely, soft crust and allow the oats to stick.

PER SERVING (1 SLICE): CALORIES: 137; TOTAL FAT: 3G; SATURATED FAT: 2G; CARBOHYDRATES: 25G; FIBER: 1G; SODIUM: 112MG; PROTEIN: 3G

Whole-Wheat Buttermilk Bread

PREP TIME IS 10 MINUTES OR LESS

This loaf of bread rises high and has an airy texture that's perfect for breakfast or a lunch box sandwich. It also offers up plenty of healthy fiber. You can substitute regular milk or water for the buttermilk if you don't happen to have any buttermilk in your refrigerator.

8 SLICES / 1 POUND	12 SLICES / 1½ POUNDS	16 SLICES / 2 POUNDS
⅔ cup buttermilk, at 80°F to 90°F	¾ cup plus 3 tablespoons buttermilk, at 80°F to 90°F	1¼ cups buttermilk, at 80°F to 90°F
1 tablespoon melted butter, cooled	1½ tablespoons melted butter, cooled	2 tablespoons melted butter, cooled
1 tablespoon honey	1½ tablespoons honey	2 tablespoons honey
¾ cup whole-wheat flour	¾ teaspoon salt	1 teaspoon salt
1¼ cups white bread flour	1⅛ cups whole-wheat flour	1½ cups whole-wheat flour
1⅛ teaspoons bread machine or instant yeast	1¾ cups plus 1 tablespoon white bread flour	2½ cups white bread flour
	1⅔ teaspoons bread machine or instant yeast	2¼ teaspoons bread machine or instant yeast

1. Place the ingredients in your bread machine as recommended by the manufacturer.

2. Program the machine for Basic/White bread, select light or medium crust, and press Start.

3. When the loaf is done, remove the bucket from the machine.

4. Let the loaf cool for 5 minutes.

5. Gently shake the bucket to remove the loaf, and turn it out onto a rack to cool.

Cooking tip: It is important to cool the melted butter to 90°F or less so that the heat does not affect the ability of the yeast to work. Make sure you use both the clarified part of the melted butter and milk solids to get the correct balance.

PER SERVING (1 SLICE): CALORIES: 135; TOTAL FAT: 2G; SATURATED FAT: 1G; CARBOHYDRATES: 25G; FIBER: 1G; SODIUM: 180MG; PROTEIN: 4G

Soft Egg Bread

PREP TIME IS 10 MINUTES OR LESS

This might become the loaf that you make over and over again because it is simple, delicious, and versatile. You need very few ingredients, and the ones in the recipe are products you probably have on hand all the time. This is also a good loaf to experiment with if you want to try adding spices or dried fruit or nuts.

8 SLICES / 1 POUND

½ cup plus 2 tablespoons milk, at 80°F to 90°F

2⅔ tablespoons melted butter, cooled

1 egg, at room temperature

2⅔ tablespoons sugar

1 teaspoon salt

2 cups white bread flour

¾ teaspoon bread machine or instant yeast

12 SLICES / 1½ POUNDS

¾ cup milk, at 80°F to 90°F

¼ cup melted butter, cooled

2 eggs, at room temperature

¼ cup sugar

1½ teaspoons salt

3 cups white bread flour

1 teaspoon bread machine or instant yeast

16 SLICES / 2 POUNDS

1 cup milk, at 80°F to 90°F

5 tablespoons melted butter, cooled

3 eggs, at room temperature

⅓ cup sugar

2 teaspoons salt

4 cups white bread flour

1½ teaspoons bread machine or instant yeast

1. Place the ingredients in your bread machine as recommended by the manufacturer.
2. Program the machine for Basic/White bread, select light or medium crust, and press Start.
3. When the loaf is done, remove the bucket from the machine.
4. Let the loaf cool for 5 minutes.
5. Gently shake the bucket to remove the loaf, and turn it out onto a rack to cool.

Substitution tip: Honey, maple syrup, or light brown sugar can all be used to sweeten this loaf instead of sugar. Use the same amount and add it to the wet ingredients.

PER SERVING (1 SLICE): CALORIES: 184; TOTAL FAT: 5G; SATURATED FAT: 3G; CARBOHYDRATES: 29G; FIBER: 1G; SODIUM: 338MG; PROTEIN: 5G

Healthy Bran Bread

PREP TIME IS 10 MINUTES OR LESS

This is not a delicate loaf with an airy texture and mild flavor—bran is rustic and strong-flavored. If you are committed to a healthy lifestyle and getting fiber in your diet, this is the perfect bread to eat for breakfast or use for a sandwich at lunch. Pile on salmon salad or leftover chicken breast for a nutrition-packed meal.

8 SLICES / 1 POUND	12 SLICES / 1½ POUNDS	16 SLICES / 2 POUNDS
¾ cup milk, at 80°F to 90°F	1⅛ cups milk, at 80°F to 90°F	1½ cups milk, at 80°F to 90°F
1½ tablespoons melted butter, cooled	2¼ tablespoons melted butter, cooled	3 tablespoons melted butter, cooled
2 tablespoons sugar	3 tablespoons sugar	¼ cup sugar
1 teaspoon salt	1½ teaspoons salt	2 teaspoons salt
¼ cup wheat bran	⅓ cup wheat bran	½ cup wheat bran
1¾ cups white bread flour	2⅔ cups white bread flour	3½ cups white bread flour
1 teaspoon bread machine or instant yeast	1½ teaspoon bread machine or instant yeast	2 teaspoons bread machine or instant yeast

1. Place the ingredients in your bread machine as recommended by the manufacturer.

2. Program the machine for Basic/White bread, select light or medium crust, and press Start.

3. When the loaf is done, remove the bucket from the machine.

4. Let the loaf cool for 5 minutes.

5. Gently shake the bucket to remove the loaf, and turn it out onto a rack to cool.

Substitution tip: Honey and dark maple syrup taste wonderful with bran, so feel free to use these sweeteners instead of sugar. Use the same amount added to the wet ingredients.

PER SERVING (1 SLICE): CALORIES: 146; TOTAL FAT: 3G; SATURATED FAT: 2G; CARBOHYDRATES: 26G; FIBER: 2G; SODIUM: 316MG; PROTEIN: 4G

Dark Rye Bread

PREP TIME IS 10 MINUTES OR LESS

Rye bread is the foundation of many famous and popular sandwiches. It can stand up to being toasted, baked, grilled, and stuffed with layers of ingredients, including juicy sauerkraut or ripe tomatoes. Some of the most familiar rye sandwiches are the Reuben, Montreal smoked meat, and pastrami.

8 SLICES / 1 POUND	12 SLICES / 1½ POUNDS	16 SLICES / 2 POUNDS
⅔ cup water, at 80°F to 90°F	1 cup water, at 80°F to 90°F	1¼ cups water, at 80°F to 90°F
1 tablespoon melted butter, cooled	1½ tablespoons melted butter, cooled	2 tablespoons melted butter, cooled
¼ cup molasses	⅓ cup molasses	½ cup molasses
¼ teaspoon salt	⅓ teaspoon salt	½ teaspoon salt
1 tablespoon unsweetened cocoa powder	1½ tablespoons unsweetened cocoa powder	2 tablespoons unsweetened cocoa powder
Pinch ground nutmeg	Pinch ground nutmeg	Pinch ground nutmeg
½ cup rye flour	¾ cup rye flour	1 cup rye flour
1¼ cups white bread flour	2 cups white bread flour	2½ cups white bread flour
1⅛ teaspoons bread machine or instant yeast	1⅔ teaspoons bread machine or instant yeast	2¼ teaspoons bread machine or instant yeast

1. Place the ingredients in your bread machine as recommended by the manufacturer.
2. Program the machine for Basic/White bread, select light or medium crust, and press Start.
3. When the loaf is done, remove the bucket from the machine.
4. Let the loaf cool for 5 minutes.
5. Gently shake the bucket to remove the loaf, and turn it out onto a rack to cool.

Ingredient tip: The cocoa powder in this recipe does not specify Dutch-process or regular-type cocoa powder. The Dutch-process cocoa is treated with an alkalizing agent so that it is less acidic and has a stronger chocolate taste. The cocoa in rye bread is meant to add color more than flavor, so using regular cocoa powder is fine.

PER SERVING (1 SLICE): CALORIES: 144; TOTAL FAT: 2G; SATURATED FAT: 1G; CARBOHYDRATES: 29G; FIBER: 3G; SODIUM: 241MG; PROTEIN: 4G

Golden Raisin Bread

PREP TIME IS 10 MINUTES OR LESS

A hint of cinnamon elevates this pretty raisin-studded bread to almost fine-dining status, especially when toasted and slathered with apple butter. You might be tempted to add more raisins than the recipe calls for, but too many can impede the rise and texture of the finished bread.

8 SLICES / 1 POUND

¾ cup milk, at 80°F to 90°F

1 tablespoon melted butter, cooled

1 tablespoon sugar

¾ teaspoon salt

½ teaspoon ground cinnamon

2 cups white bread flour

1 teaspoon bread machine or instant yeast

½ cup golden raisins

12 SLICES / 1½ POUNDS

1⅛ cups milk, at 80°F to 90°F

1½ tablespoons melted butter, cooled

2 tablespoons sugar

1 teaspoon salt

¾ teaspoon ground cinnamon

3 cups white bread flour

1½ teaspoons bread machine or instant yeast

¾ cup golden raisins

16 SLICES / 2 POUNDS

1½ cups milk, at 80°F to 90°F

2 tablespoons melted butter, cooled

3 tablespoons sugar

1½ teaspoons salt

1 teaspoon ground cinnamon

4 cups white bread flour

2 teaspoons bread machine or instant yeast

1 cup golden raisins

1. Place the ingredients, except the raisins, in your bread machine as recommended by the manufacturer.
2. Program the machine for Basic/White or Sweet bread, select light or medium crust, and press Start.
3. Add the raisins at the raisin/nut signal.
4. When the loaf is done, remove the bucket from the machine.
5. Let the loaf cool for 5 minutes.
6. Gently shake the bucket to remove the loaf, and turn it out onto a rack to cool.

Cooking tip: Do not add the raisins at the beginning with all the other ingredients, because the paddles will tear the dried fruit apart. If you do not have a raisin/nut signal on your machine, wait until 5 to 10 minutes before the last kneading cycle ends.

PER SERVING (1 SLICE): CALORIES: 173; TOTAL FAT: 3G; SATURATED FAT: 1G; CARBOHYDRATES: 34G; FIBER: 1G; SODIUM: 216MG; PROTEIN: 4G

Golden Corn Bread

PREP TIME IS 10 MINUTES OR LESS

Corn bread is served in large chunks alongside many of the spicy dishes found in South America and the southern United States. It can be difficult to decide if corn bread is a true bread or dessert because the texture is dense and its flavor is often sweet. Try adding bacon bits or Cheddar to this base recipe for an interesting variation.

12 TO 16 SLICES / 1 ½ TO 2 POUNDS

1 cup buttermilk, at 80°F to 90°F

¼ cup melted butter, cooled

2 eggs, at room temperature

1⅓ cups all-purpose flour

1 cup cornmeal

¼ cup sugar

1 tablespoon baking powder

1 teaspoon salt

1. Place the buttermilk, butter, and eggs in your in your bread machine as recommended by the manufacturer.

2. Program the machine for Quick/Rapid bread and press Start.

3. While the wet ingredients are mixing, stir together the flour, cornmeal, sugar, baking powder, and salt in a small bowl.

4. After the first fast mixing is done and the machine signals, add the dry ingredients.

5. When the loaf is done, remove the bucket from the machine.

6. Let the loaf cool for 5 minutes.

7. Gently shake the bucket to remove the loaf, and turn it out onto a rack to cool.

Machine tip: This loaf is perfectly done in a 1½-pound machine, but it can be made in a 1-pound and 2-pound machine as well. If you are using a 2-pound machine, the loaf will be shorter, and it would be a good idea to take the paddles out after the mixing cycle is complete.

PER SERVING (1 SLICE): CALORIES: 158; TOTAL FAT: 5G; SATURATED FAT: 3G; CARBOHYDRATES: 24G; FIBER: 1G; SODIUM: 259MG; PROTEIN: 4G

English Muffin Bread

PREP TIME IS 10 MINUTES OR LESS

Although this bread does not have the tiny holes that characterize English muffins, the taste is quite similar. You will find that even in a light crust setting, the crust is firm and the texture of the bread is dense. The addition of baking soda helps give it the exact right taste to mimic its namesake.

8 SLICES / 1 POUND	12 SLICES / 1½ POUNDS	16 SLICES / 2 POUNDS
⅔ cup buttermilk, at 80°F to 90°F	1¼ cups buttermilk, at 80°F to 90°F	1¼ cups buttermilk, at 80°F to 90°F
1 tablespoon melted butter, cooled	1½ tablespoons melted butter, cooled	2 tablespoons melted butter, cooled
1 tablespoon sugar	1½ tablespoons sugar	2 tablespoons sugar
¾ teaspoon salt	1⅛ teaspoons salt	1½ teaspoons salt
¼ teaspoon baking powder	⅓ teaspoon baking powder	½ teaspoon baking powder
1¾ cups white bread flour	2⅔ cups white bread flour	3½ cups white bread flour
1⅛ teaspoons bread machine or instant yeast	1⅔ teaspoons bread machine or instant yeast	2¼ teaspoons bread machine or instant yeast

1. Place the ingredients in your bread machine as recommended by the manufacturer.

2. Program the machine for Basic/White bread, select light or medium crust, and press Start.

3. When the loaf is done, remove the bucket from the machine.

4. Let the loaf cool for 5 minutes.

5. Gently shake the bucket to remove the loaf, and turn it out onto a rack to cool.

Decoration tip: If you want to create an authentic English muffin taste, remove the dough from the machine after the kneading cycle is complete, and roll the dough ball in cornmeal. Place the ball back in the bucket and let the machine continue its rise and bake cycles.

PER SERVING (1 SLICE): CALORIES: 131; TOTAL FAT: 2G; SATURATED FAT: 1G; CARBOHYDRATES: 24G; FIBER: 1G; SODIUM: 232MG; PROTEIN: 4G

Traditional Italian Bread

PREP TIME IS 10 MINUTES OR LESS

There is a certain type of bread that works well for garlic breads, bruschetta, and dipping in steaming bowls of soup. This loaf will hold up well in heat and has a mild, pleasant taste. If you are a French toast enthusiast, this is also the bread for you.

8 SLICES / 1 POUND	12 SLICES / 1 ½ POUNDS	16 SLICES / 2 POUNDS
⅔ cup water, at 80°F to 90°F	1 cup water, at 80°F to 90°F	1 ¼ cups plus 2 tablespoons water, at 80°F to 90°F
1 tablespoon olive oil	1 ½ tablespoons olive oil	2 tablespoons olive oil
1 tablespoon sugar	1 ½ tablespoons sugar	2 tablespoons sugar
¾ teaspoon salt	1 ⅛ teaspoons salt	1 ½ teaspoons salt
2 cups white bread flour	3 cups white bread flour	4 cups white bread flour
1 teaspoon bread machine or instant yeast	1 ½ teaspoons bread machine or instant yeast	2 teaspoons bread machine or instant yeast

1. Place the ingredients in your bread machine as recommended by the manufacturer.
2. Program the machine for Basic/White bread, select light or medium crust, and press Start.
3. When the loaf is done, remove the bucket from the machine.
4. Let the loaf cool for 5 minutes.
5. Gently shake the bucket to remove the loaf, and turn it out onto a rack to cool.

"Did You Know?" Italian bread, although made from similar ingredients as French bread, has a thinner crust because the yeast is allowed to rise fully. The interior of the loaf is often more absorbent and moist than French bread.

PER SERVING (1 SLICE): CALORIES: 136; TOTAL FAT: 2G; SATURATED FAT: 0G; CARBOHYDRATES: 26G; FIBER: 1G; SODIUM: 195MG; PROTEIN: 3G

—Chapter Three—

SPICE AND HERB BREADS

Fragrant Herb Bread

PREP TIME IS 10 MINUTES OR LESS

There is something sublime about the scent of herbs combined with baking bread. It makes you want to shut your eyes and let your worries float away. You can certainly add your favorite herb to this fluffy bread, and fresh herbs would also make a great addition. If you want to substitute fresh chopped herbs, double the amounts at the very least.

8 SLICES / 1 POUND	12 SLICES / 1½ POUNDS	16 SLICES / 2 POUNDS
¾ cup water, at 80°F to 90°F	1⅛ cups water, at 80°F to 90°F	1½ cups water, at 80°F to 90°F
1 tablespoon melted butter, cooled	1½ tablespoons melted butter, cooled	2 tablespoons melted butter, cooled
1 tablespoon sugar	1½ tablespoons sugar	2 tablespoons sugar
¾ teaspoon salt	1 teaspoon salt	2 teaspoons salt
2 tablespoons skim milk powder	3 tablespoons skim milk powder	¼ cup skim milk powder
1 teaspoon dried thyme	1 teaspoon dried thyme	2 teaspoons dried thyme
1 teaspoon dried chives	1 teaspoon dried chives	2 teaspoons dried chives
½ teaspoon dried oregano	1 teaspoon dried oregano	1 teaspoon dried oregano
2 cups white bread flour	3 cups white bread flour	4 cups white bread flour
¾ teaspoon bread machine or instant yeast	1¼ teaspoons bread machine or instant yeast	1¼ teaspoons bread machine or instant yeast

1. Place the ingredients in your bread machine as recommended by the manufacturer.
2. Program the machine for Basic/White bread, select light or medium crust, and press Start.
3. When the loaf is done, remove the bucket from the machine.
4. Let the loaf cool for 5 minutes.
5. Gently shake the bucket to remove the loaf, and turn it out onto a rack to cool.

"Did You Know?" Thyme is an herb commonly used, fresh or dried, in Mediterranean cooking. It's packed with nutrition, including health-promoting phytonutrients (plant-derived compounds), antioxidants, B-complex vitamins, and vitamin C.

PER SERVING (1 SLICE): CALORIES: 141; TOTAL FAT: 2G; SATURATED FAT: 1G; CARBOHYDRATES: 27G; FIBER: 1G; SODIUM: 215MG; PROTEIN: 4G

Rosemary Bread

The scent of rosemary will waft throughout your entire house while this bread bakes, and you might find yourself waiting impatiently with a tub of butter for it to be finished. Rosemary is one of the stronger-smelling herbs, especially if the needles are very fresh. The flavor lends itself well to thick sandwiches made with rare roast beef or roasted turkey breast with mayonnaise.

8 SLICES / 1 POUND	12 SLICES / 1½ POUNDS	16 SLICES / 2 POUNDS
¾ cup plus 1 tablespoon water, at 80°F to 90°F	1¼ cups water, at 80°F to 90°F	2⅓ cups water, at 80°F to 90°F
1⅔ tablespoons melted butter, cooled	2½ tablespoons melted butter, cooled	3⅓ tablespoons melted butter, cooled
2 teaspoons sugar	1 tablespoon sugar	4 teaspoons sugar
1 teaspoon salt	1½ teaspoons salt	2 teaspoons salt
1 tablespoon finely chopped fresh rosemary	1½ tablespoons finely chopped fresh rosemary	2 tablespoons finely chopped fresh rosemary
2 cups white bread flour	3 cups white bread flour	4 cups white bread flour
1⅓ teaspoons bread machine or instant yeast	2 teaspoons bread machine or instant yeast	2¼ teaspoons bread machine or instant yeast

1. Place the ingredients in your bread machine as recommended by the manufacturer.
2. Program the machine for Basic/White bread, select light or medium crust, and press Start.
3. When the loaf is done, remove the bucket from the machine.
4. Let the loaf cool for 5 minutes.
5. Gently shake the bucket to remove the loaf, and turn it out onto a rack to cool.

Ingredient tip: If you are not a fan of bits of chopped rosemary in your bread, try infusing the water in the recipe instead. Pour a little more than the required amount of water in a saucepan with the chopped rosemary. Simmer the liquid for at least 15 minutes, strain out the herbs, and cool the water to the correct temperature for bread making.

PER SERVING (1 SLICE): CALORIES: 142; TOTAL FAT: 3G; SATURATED FAT: 2G; CARBOHYDRATES: 25G; FIBER: 1G; SODIUM: 309MG; PROTEIN: 4G

Spicy Cajun Bread

PREP TIME IS 10 MINUTES OR LESS

For a Cajun sandwich, what could be more appropriate than red-tinted bread with just enough heat to perk up your senses? Cajun spice is complex because it is a combination of many other spices, including red chili flakes. If you want spicier bread, look for a spice with a greater amount of chili.

8 SLICES / 1 POUND	12 SLICES / 1½ POUNDS	16 SLICES / 2 POUNDS
¾ cup water, at 80°F to 90°F	1⅛ cups water, at 80°F to 90°F	1½ cups water, at 80°F to 90°F
1 tablespoon melted butter, cooled	1½ tablespoons melted butter, cooled	2 tablespoons melted butter, cooled
2 teaspoons tomato paste	1 tablespoon tomato paste	1 tablespoon tomato paste
1 tablespoon sugar	1½ tablespoons sugar	2 tablespoons sugar
1 teaspoon salt	1½ teaspoons salt	2 teaspoons salt
2 tablespoons skim milk powder	3 tablespoons skim milk powder	¼ cup skim milk powder
½ tablespoon Cajun seasoning	¾ tablespoon Cajun seasoning	1 tablespoon Cajun seasoning
⅛ teaspoon onion powder	¼ teaspoon onion powder	¼ teaspoon onion powder
2 cups white bread flour	3 cups white bread flour	4 cups white bread flour
1 teaspoon bread machine or instant yeast	1¼ teaspoons bread machine or instant yeast	1¼ teaspoons bread machine or instant yeast

1. Place the ingredients in your bread machine as recommended by the manufacturer.
2. Program the machine for Basic/White bread, select light or medium crust, and press Start.
3. When the loaf is done, remove the bucket from the machine.
4. Let the loaf cool for 5 minutes.
5. Gently shake the bucket to remove the loaf, and turn it out onto a rack to cool.

Cooking tip: To ensure a uniform reddish tint in this bread, stir the tomato paste into the water before adding all the other ingredients.

PER SERVING (1 SLICE): CALORIES: 141; TOTAL FAT: 2G; SATURATED FAT: 1G; CARBOHYDRATES: 27G; FIBER: 1G; SODIUM: 323MG; PROTEIN: 4G

Aromatic Lavender Bread

PREP TIME IS 10 MINUTES OR LESS

Known for its pretty purple flowers, lavender has long been used for culinary purposes. You can purchase it dried or grow culinary lavender yourself and enjoy the fragrant scent in your home. If you want to make this bread in the winter when lavender flowers are scarce, substitute chopped fresh thyme because it has a similar flavor.

8 SLICES / 1 POUND	12 SLICES / 1 ½ POUNDS	16 SLICES / 2 POUNDS
¾ cup milk, at 80°F to 90°F	1⅛ cups milk, at 80°F to 90°F	1½ cups milk, at 80°F to 90°F
1 tablespoon melted butter, cooled	1½ tablespoons melted butter, cooled	2 tablespoons melted butter, cooled
1 tablespoon sugar	1½ tablespoons sugar	2 tablespoons sugar
¾ teaspoon salt	1 teaspoon salt	2 teaspoons salt
1 teaspoon chopped fresh lavender flowers	1½ teaspoons chopped fresh lavender flowers	2 teaspoons chopped fresh lavender flowers
¼ teaspoon lemon zest	½ teaspoon lemon zest	1 teaspoon lemon zest
¼ teaspoon chopped fresh thyme	½ teaspoon chopped fresh thyme	½ teaspoon chopped fresh thyme
2 cups white bread flour	3 cups white bread flour	4 cups white bread flour
¾ teaspoon bread machine or instant yeast	1¼ teaspoons bread machine or instant yeast	1½ teaspoons bread machine or instant yeast

1. Place the ingredients in your bread machine as recommended by the manufacturer.
2. Program the machine for Basic/White bread, select light or medium crust, and press Start.
3. When the loaf is done, remove the bucket from the machine.
4. Let the loaf cool for 5 minutes.
5. Gently shake the bucket to remove the loaf, and turn it out onto a rack to cool.

Decoration tip: Drizzle a little glaze made from milk, confectioners' sugar, and vanilla over this bread when it is completely cooled. Cut the bread into even slices and arrange them on a plate with lavender sprigs for a stunning lunch treat.

PER SERVING (1 SLICE): CALORIES: 144; TOTAL FAT: 2G; SATURATED FAT: 1G; CARBOHYDRATES: 27G; FIBER: 1G; SODIUM: 214MG; PROTEIN: 4G

Cracked Black Pepper Bread

PREP TIME IS 10 MINUTES OR LESS

Cracked pepper is completely different than the finely ground spice that is found in most pantries at home and set on restaurant tables in handy shakers. Professional chefs often crack black peppercorns just before service to ensure a pungent, intense flavor. This is done by pouring whole black peppercorns on a hard surface and using the back of a skillet to grind the kernels into uneven pieces.

8 SLICES / 1 POUND

¾ cup water, at 80°F to 90°F

1 tablespoon melted butter, cooled

1 tablespoon sugar

¾ teaspoon salt

2 tablespoons skim milk powder

1 tablespoon minced chives

½ teaspoon garlic powder

½ teaspoon cracked black pepper

2 cups white bread flour

¾ teaspoon bread machine or instant yeast

12 SLICES / 1½ POUNDS

1⅛ cups water, at 80°F to 90°F

1½ tablespoons melted butter, cooled

1½ tablespoons sugar

1 teaspoon salt

3 tablespoons skim milk powder

1½ tablespoons minced chives

¾ teaspoon garlic powder

¾ teaspoon freshly cracked black pepper

3 cups white bread flour

1¼ teaspoons bread machine or instant yeast

16 SLICES / 2 POUNDS

1½ cups water, at 80°F to 90°F

2 tablespoons melted butter, cooled

2 tablespoons sugar

2 teaspoons salt

¼ cup skim milk powder

2 tablespoons minced chives

1 teaspoon garlic powder

1 teaspoon freshly cracked black pepper

4 cups white bread flour

1½ teaspoons bread machine or instant yeast

1. Place the ingredients in your bread machine as recommended by the manufacturer.

2. Program the machine for Basic/White bread, select light or medium crust, and press Start.

3. When the loaf is done, remove the bucket from the machine.

4. Let the loaf cool for 5 minutes.

5. Gently shake the bucket to remove the loaf, and turn it out onto a rack to cool.

Ingredient tip: You can buy cracked black pepper in the supermarket in the spice aisle if you don't have the time or inclination to crack your own. This pepper product will not be as strong or as fresh, but you will still taste the flavor kick in the bread.

PER SERVING (1 SLICE): CALORIES: 141; TOTAL FAT: 2G; SATURATED FAT: 1G; CARBOHYDRATES: 27G; FIBER: 1G; SODIUM: 215MG; PROTEIN: 4G

Herb and Garlic Cream Cheese Bread

PREP TIME IS 10 MINUTES OR LESS

This bread is tender, lightly herbal, and perfect for toasted tomato or cucumber sandwiches. It cannot be kept for a prolonged period of time at room temperature, because it contains dairy products and no preservatives are used. When the loaf is cooled, seal it in a freezer bag and store it in the refrigerator.

8 SLICES / 1 POUND	12 SLICES / 1 ½ POUNDS	16 SLICES / 2 POUNDS
⅓ cup water, at 80°F to 90°F	½ cup water, at 80°F to 90°F	⅔ cup water, at 80°F to 90°F
⅓ cup herb and garlic cream cheese, at room temperature	½ cup herb and garlic cream cheese, at room temperature	⅔ cup herb and garlic cream cheese, at room temperature
1 egg, at room temperature	1 egg, at room temperature	1 egg, at room temperature
4 teaspoons melted butter, cooled	2 tablespoons melted butter, cooled	2⅔ tablespoons melted butter, cooled
1 tablespoon sugar	3 tablespoons sugar	¼ cup sugar
⅔ teaspoon salt	1 teaspoon salt	1⅓ teaspoons salt
2 cups white bread flour	3 cups white bread flour	4 cups white bread flour
1 teaspoon bread machine or instant yeast	1½ teaspoons bread machine or instant yeast	2 teaspoons bread machine or instant yeast

1. Place the ingredients in your bread machine as recommended by the manufacturer.

2. Program the machine for Basic/White bread, select light or medium crust, and press Start.

3. When the loaf is done, remove the bucket from the machine.

4. Let the loaf cool for 5 minutes.

5. Gently shake the bucket to remove the loaf, and turn it out onto a rack to cool.

Variation tip: Plain, garlic, or smoked salmon cream cheese would all be delightful choices in this recipe to create interesting varieties of bread. Do not use low-fat or nonfat products when making this loaf.

PER SERVING (1 SLICE): CALORIES: 182; TOTAL FAT: 6G; SATURATED FAT: 3G; CARBOHYDRATES: 27G; FIBER: 1G; SODIUM: 242MG; PROTEIN: 5G

Honey-Spice Egg Bread

PREP TIME IS 10 MINUTES OR LESS

Egg bread has a glorious golden color and an almost flaky texture that might be familiar if you enjoy challah. This bread is not braided into an intricate loaf, but it can still be sliced and nicely displayed for a special family event. Try using egg bread for French toast for a truly sublime culinary experience.

8 SLICES / 1 POUND	12 SLICES / 1½ POUNDS	16 SLICES / 2 POUNDS
¾ cup milk, at 80°F to 90°F	1 cup milk, at 80°F to 90°F	1⅓ cup milk, at 80°F to 90°F
1 egg, at room temperature	2 eggs, at room temperature	2 eggs, at room temperature
1 tablespoon melted butter, cooled	1½ tablespoons melted butter, cooled	2 tablespoons melted butter, cooled
4 teaspoons honey	2 tablespoons honey	2⅔ tablespoons honey
⅔ teaspoon salt	1 teaspoon salt	1⅓ teaspoons salt
⅔ teaspoon ground cinnamon	1 teaspoon ground cinnamon	1⅓ teaspoons ground cinnamon
⅓ teaspoon ground cardamom	½ teaspoon ground cardamom	⅔ teaspoon ground cardamom
⅓ teaspoon ground nutmeg	½ teaspoon ground nutmeg	⅔ teaspoon ground nutmeg
2 cups white bread flour	3 cups white bread flour	4 cups white bread flour
1⅓ teaspoons bread machine or instant yeast	2 teaspoons bread machine or instant yeast	2¼ teaspoons bread machine or instant yeast

1. Place the ingredients in your bread machine as recommended by the manufacturer.
2. Program the machine for Basic/White bread, select light or medium crust, and press Start.
3. When the loaf is done, remove the bucket from the machine.
4. Let the loaf cool for 5 minutes.
5. Gently shake the bucket to remove the loaf, and turn it out onto a rack to cool.

Ingredient tip: Cardamom has a citrusy, almost smoky aroma and is a member of the ginger family. Most of the cardamom found in grocery stores is ground-up black cardamom, which is less expensive than green cardamom, one of the most costly spices in the world.

PER SERVING (1 SLICE): CALORIES: 162; TOTAL FAT: 3G; SATURATED FAT: 2G; CARBOHYDRATES: 28G; FIBER: 1G; SODIUM: 226MG; PROTEIN: 5G

Cinnamon Bread

PREP TIME IS 10 MINUTES OR LESS

Who doesn't remember getting delicious cinnamon toast as a child, served fragrant and warm when you needed a morning pick-me-up before school? This bread is an all-in-one that just requires you to pop a slice in the toaster and add a little sweet butter when it is golden brown. Other warm spices, such as nutmeg or ginger, can also be added in pinches to the recipe to create a more complex flavor.

8 SLICES / 1 POUND	12 SLICES / 1½ POUNDS	16 SLICES / 2 POUNDS
⅔ cup milk, at 80°F to 90°F	1 cup milk, at 80°F to 90°F	1⅔ cup milk, at 80°F to 90°F
1 egg, at room temperature	1 egg, at room temperature	1 egg, at room temperature
3 tablespoons melted butter, cooled	¼ cup melted butter, cooled	⅓ cup melted butter, cooled
⅓ cup sugar	½ cup sugar	⅔ cup sugar
⅓ teaspoon salt	½ teaspoon salt	⅔ teaspoon salt
1 teaspoon ground cinnamon	1½ teaspoons ground cinnamon	2 teaspoons ground cinnamon
2 cups white bread flour	3 cups white bread flour	4 cups white bread flour
1⅓ teaspoons bread machine or active dry yeast	2 teaspoons bread machine or active dry yeast	2¼ teaspoons bread machine or active dry yeast

1. Place the ingredients in your bread machine as recommended by the manufacturer.
2. Program the machine for Basic/White bread, select light or medium crust, and press Start.
3. When the loaf is done, remove the bucket from the machine.
4. Let the loaf cool for 5 minutes.
5. Gently shake the bucket to remove the loaf, and turn it out onto a rack to cool.

"Did You Know?" Cinnamon is one spice that is used both in Eastern (including Indian) and Western cuisines. In the West, cinnamon is most commonly used in preparing sweet dishes, such as desserts and pies (and bread!). In India, it is most often used in curries, biryanis, and vegetable dishes.

PER SERVING (1 SLICE): CALORIES: 198; TOTAL FAT: 5G; SATURATED FAT: 3G; CARBOHYDRATES: 34G; FIBER: 1G; SODIUM: 141MG; PROTEIN: 5G

Simple Garlic Bread

PREP TIME IS 10 MINUTES OR LESS

Any meats, tuna salad, or grilled vegetable creations will taste amazing between thick slices of this garlic-scented loaf. The garlic flavor is subtle, and the texture is similar to Italian bread without the hard crust. Try a little garlic mayonnaise on the bread if you want to double up on the garlic taste.

8 SLICES / 1 POUND	12 SLICES / 1½ POUNDS	16 SLICES / 2 POUNDS
⅔ cup milk, at 70°F to 80°F°	1 cup milk, at 70°F to 80°F	1⅓ cup milk, at 70°F to 80°F
1 tablespoon melted butter, cooled	1½ tablespoons melted butter, cooled	2 tablespoons melted butter, cooled
2 teaspoons sugar	1 tablespoon sugar	4 teaspoons sugar
1 teaspoon salt	1½ teaspoons salt	2 teaspoons salt
1⅓ teaspoons garlic powder	2 teaspoons garlic powder	2⅔ teaspoons garlic powder
1⅓ teaspoons chopped fresh parsley	2 teaspoons chopped fresh parsley	2⅔ teaspoons chopped fresh parsley
2 cups white bread flour	3 cups white bread flour	4 cups white bread flour
1⅛ teaspoons bread machine or instant yeast	1¾ teaspoons bread machine or instant yeast	2¼ teaspoons bread machine or instant yeast

1. Place the ingredients in your bread machine as recommended by the manufacturer.
2. Program the machine for Basic/White bread, select light or medium crust, and press Start.
3. When the loaf is done, remove the bucket from the machine.
4. Let the loaf cool for 5 minutes.
5. Gently shake the bucket to remove the loaf, and turn it out onto a rack to cool.

Substitution tip: Minced garlic can be substituted for the garlic powder. Add the fresh garlic to the wet ingredients in the same amount as the powdered garlic.

PER SERVING (1 SLICE): CALORIES: 144; TOTAL FAT: 2G; SATURATED FAT: 1G; CARBOHYDRATES: 26G; FIBER: 1G; SODIUM: 312MG; PROTEIN: 4G

Herbed Pesto Bread

PREP TIME IS 10 MINUTES OR LESS

Pesto is a versatile condiment that is created with many different ingredients, such as herbs, greens, sun-dried tomatoes, nuts, cheese, and oil. The "pesto" here is in the form of the usual ingredients added individually into the bread. If you'd like, you can swap the amounts of the parsley and basil so the basil is a stronger flavor.

8 SLICES / 1 POUND	12 SLICES / 1½ POUNDS	16 SLICES / 2 POUNDS
⅔ cup water, at 80°F to 90°F	1 cup water, at 80°F to 90°F	1¼ cups water, at 80°F to 90°F
1½ tablespoons melted butter, cooled	2¼ tablespoons melted butter, cooled	3 tablespoons melted butter, cooled
1 teaspoon minced garlic	1½ teaspoons minced garlic	2 teaspoons minced garlic
½ tablespoon sugar	¾ tablespoon sugar	1 tablespoon sugar
¾ teaspoon salt	1 teaspoon salt	1¼ teaspoons salt
2 tablespoons chopped fresh parsley	3 tablespoons chopped fresh parsley	¼ cup chopped fresh parsley
¾ teaspoon chopped fresh basil	1½ tablespoons chopped fresh basil	2 tablespoons chopped fresh basil
¼ cup grated Parmesan cheese	⅓ cup grated Parmesan cheese	½ cup (2 ounces) grated Parmesan cheese
2 cups white bread flour	3 cups white bread flour	4 cups white bread flour
¾ teaspoon bread machine or active dry yeast	1¼ teaspoons bread machine or active dry yeast	1½ teaspoons bread machine or active dry yeast

1. Place the ingredients in your bread machine as recommended by the manufacturer.

2. Program the machine for Basic/White bread, select light or medium crust, and press Start.

3. When the loaf is done, remove the bucket from the machine.

4. Let the loaf cool for 5 minutes.

5. Gently shake the bucket to remove the loaf, and turn it out onto a rack to cool.

Decoration tip: Shredded Parmesan or Asiago cheese can be sprinkled on the finished loaf right after you pop it out of the bucket.

PER SERVING (1 SLICE): CALORIES: 149; TOTAL FAT: 3G; SATURATED FAT: 2G; CARBOHYDRATES: 25G; FIBER: 1G; SODIUM: 243MG; PROTEIN: 5G

Caraway Rye Bread

PREP TIME IS 10 MINUTES OR LESS

Caraway seeds are a common additive to rye bread because the strong flavor of the spice does not overwhelm the robust texture and taste of rye. Caraway is a member of the parsley family and has a sweet, slightly peppery aroma. The spice is often used in savory dishes, including cabbage soup, sauerkraut, and salads, but it is also delicious when added to breads, cakes, biscuits, and cheese.

8 SLICES / 1 POUND	12 SLICES / 1 ½ POUNDS	16 SLICES / 2 POUNDS
¾ cup water, at 80°F to 90°F	1⅛ cups water, at 80°F to 90°F	1½ cups water, at 80°F to 90°F
1¼ tablespoons melted butter, cooled	1¾ tablespoons melted butter, cooled	2½ tablespoons melted butter, cooled
2 tablespoons dark brown sugar	3 tablespoons dark brown sugar	¼ cup dark brown sugar
1 tablespoon dark molasses	1½ tablespoons dark molasses	2 tablespoons dark molasses
¾ teaspoon salt	1⅛ teaspoons salt	1½ teaspoons salt
1 teaspoon caraway seeds	1½ teaspoons caraway seed	2 teaspoons caraway seeds
½ cup dark rye flour	¾ cup dark rye flour	1 cup dark rye flour
1⅓ cups white bread flour	2 cups white bread flour	2¾ cups white bread flour
¾ teaspoon bread machine or instant yeast	1⅛ teaspoons bread machine or instant yeast	1½ teaspoons bread machine or instant yeast

1. Place the ingredients in your bread machine as recommended by the manufacturer.
2. Program the machine for Basic/White bread, select light or medium crust, and press Start.
3. When the loaf is done, remove the bucket from the machine.
4. Let the loaf cool for 5 minutes.
5. Gently shake the bucket to remove the loaf, and turn it out onto a rack to cool.

Decoration tip: After removing the loaf from the bread machine, brush it generously with melted butter to create a softer crust and lovely sheen.

PER SERVING (1 SLICE): CALORIES: 134; TOTAL FAT: 2G; SATURATED FAT: 1G; CARBOHYDRATES: 26G; FIBER: 3G; SODIUM: 208MG; PROTEIN: 4G

Anise Lemon Bread

PREP TIME IS 10 MINUTES OR LESS

Anise is the most prevalent flavor in this bread with just a hint of complementary citrus to tease the palate. Cream cheese and cucumber slices would make an inspired filling for sandwiches made with the bread. Try this sandwich combination for your next spring luncheon or for a child's tea party.

8 SLICES / 1 POUND	12 SLICES / 1½ POUNDS	16 SLICES / 2 POUNDS
⅔ cup water, at 80°F to 90°F	¾ cup water, at 80°F to 90°F	1 cup plus 1 tablespoon water, at 80°F to 90°F
1 egg, at room temperature	1 egg, at room temperature	1 egg, at room temperature
2⅔ tablespoons butter, melted and cooled	¼ cup butter, melted and cooled	⅓ cup butter, melted and cooled
2⅔ tablespoons honey	¼ cup honey	⅓ cup honey
⅓ teaspoon salt	½ teaspoon salt	⅔ teaspoon salt
⅔ teaspoon anise seed	1 teaspoon anise seed	1⅓ teaspoons anise seed
⅔ teaspoon lemon zest	1 teaspoon lemon zest	1⅓ teaspoons lemon zest
2 cups white bread flour	3 cups white bread flour	4 cups white bread flour
1⅓ teaspoons bread machine or instant yeast	2 teaspoons bread machine or instant yeast	2½ teaspoons bread machine or instant yeast

1. Place the ingredients in your bread machine as recommended by the manufacturer.

2. Program the machine for Basic/White bread, select light or medium crust, and press Start.

3. When the loaf is done, remove the bucket from the machine.

4. Let the loaf cool for 5 minutes.

5. Gently shake the bucket to remove the loaf, and turn it out onto a rack to cool.

"Did You Know?" The lovely flavor in commercially produced licorice comes from anise seed, not the actual licorice root. Anise is one of the oldest cultivated spices and was so valuable that it was taxed when imported in the 1300s in England.

PER SERVING (1 SLICE): CALORIES: 158; TOTAL FAT: 5G; SATURATED FAT: 3G; CARBOHYDRATES: 30G; FIBER: 1G; SODIUM: 131MG; PROTEIN: 4G

Fragrant Cardamom Bread

PREP TIME IS 10 MINUTES OR LESS

The scent of this bread baking will seem exotic and unfamiliar if cardamom is not a spice used regularly in your cooking repertoire. Cardamom is citrusy with a hint of ginger heat, which makes sense because these two tropical plants are related. It is easy to see why this valuable spice is called the "Queen of Spices" in India.

8 SLICES / 1 POUND	12 SLICES / 1½ POUNDS	16 SLICES / 2 POUNDS
½ cup milk, at 80°F to 90°F	¾ cup milk, at 80°F to 90°F	1 cup plus 2 tablespoons milk, at 80°F to 90°F
1 egg, at room temperature	1 egg, at room temperature	1 egg, at room temperature
1 teaspoon melted butter, cooled	1½ teaspoons melted butter, cooled	2 teaspoons melted butter, cooled
4 teaspoons honey	3 tablespoons honey	¼ cup honey
⅔ teaspoon salt	1 teaspoon salt	1⅓ teaspoons salt
⅔ teaspoon ground cardamom	1 teaspoon ground cardamom	1⅓ teaspoons ground cardamom
2 cups white bread flour	3 cups white bread flour	4 cups white bread flour
¾ teaspoon bread machine or instant yeast	1¼ teaspoons bread machine or instant yeast	1⅔ teaspoons bread machine or instant yeast

1. Place the ingredients in your bread machine as recommended by the manufacturer.
2. Program the machine for Basic/White bread, select light or medium crust, and press Start.
3. When the loaf is done, remove the bucket from the machine.
4. Let the loaf cool for 5 minutes.
5. Gently shake the bucket to remove the loaf, and turn it out onto a rack to cool.

Ingredient tip: There are three types of cardamom that can be purchased for your recipe needs: green, black, and Madagascar. Ground cardamom is the most common product in mainstream grocery stores, and it is made from green cardamom. If you want a very intense flavor, buy this spice in the pods and grind it yourself.

PER SERVING (1 SLICE): CALORIES: 149; TOTAL FAT: 2G; SATURATED FAT: 1G; CARBOHYDRATES: 29G; FIBER: 1G; SODIUM: 211MG; PROTEIN: 5G

Chocolate Mint Bread

PREP TIME IS 10 MINUTES OR LESS

The combination of chocolate and mint is used in many desserts, so why not try them in bread? With the chocolate chips, this bread is more of a treat than a healthy lunch staple, but you could pack a slice as a lunch surprise, spreading it simply with butter. You could also try dipping thick slices of this bread in egg for spectacular and unique French toast.

8 SLICES / 1 POUND	12 SLICES / 1½ POUNDS	16 SLICES / 2 POUNDS
¾ cup milk, at 80°F to 90°F	1 cup milk, at 80°F to 90°F	1¼ cups plus 2 tablespoons milk, at 80°F to 90°F
⅛ teaspoon mint extract	⅛ teaspoon mint extract	¼ teaspoon mint extract
1 tablespoon butter, melted and cooled	1½ tablespoons butter, melted and cooled	2 tablespoons butter, melted and cooled
2⅔ tablespoons sugar	¼ cup sugar	⅓ cup sugar
⅔ teaspoon salt	1 teaspoon salt	1¼ teaspoons salt
1 tablespoon unsweetened cocoa powder	1½ tablespoons unsweetened cocoa powder	2 tablespoons unsweetened cocoa powder
2 cups white bread flour	3 cups white bread flour	4 cups white bread flour
1¼ teaspoons bread machine or instant yeast	1¾ teaspoons bread machine or instant yeast	2½ teaspoons bread machine or instant yeast
⅓ cup semisweet chocolate chips	½ cup semisweet chocolate chips	¾ cup semisweet chocolate chips

1. Place the ingredients in your bread machine as recommended by the manufacturer.
2. Program the machine for Sweet bread, select light or medium crust, and press Start.
3. When the loaf is done, remove the bucket from the machine.
4. Let the loaf cool for 5 minutes.
5. Gently shake the bucket to remove the loaf, and turn it out onto a rack to cool.

Variation tip: Omit the cocoa powder and mint extract and use mint chocolate chips for a delicious and different bread, or you can use all three ingredients to double up on the mint chocolate flavor.

PER SERVING (1 SLICE): CALORIES: 177; TOTAL FAT: 3G; SATURATED FAT: 2G; CARBOHYDRATES: 32G; FIBER: 1G; SODIUM: 230MG; PROTEIN: 4G

Molasses Candied-Ginger Bread

PREP TIME IS 10 MINUTES OR LESS

This bread is basically oatmeal bread spiked with molasses and hot ginger. As with other breads made with oatmeal, the texture is a bit denser and the flavor slightly sweeter. Try a slice toasted with butter and a generous spreading of marmalade.

8 SLICES / 1 POUND	12 SLICES / 1 ½ POUNDS	16 SLICES / 2 POUNDS
⅔ cup milk, at 80°F to 90°F	1 cup milk, at 80°F to 90°F	1⅓ cups milk, at 80°F to 90°F
1 egg, at room temperature	1 egg, at room temperature	1 egg, at room temperature
2⅔ tablespoons dark molasses	¼ cup dark molasses	⅓ cup dark molasses
4 teaspoons butter, melted and cooled	3 tablespoons butter, melted and cooled	¼ cup butter, melted and cooled
⅓ teaspoon salt	½ teaspoon salt	⅔ teaspoon salt
2⅔ tablespoons chopped candied ginger	¼ cup chopped candied ginger	⅓ cup chopped candied ginger
⅓ cup quick oats	½ cup quick oats	⅔ cup quick oats
2 cups white bread flour	3 cups white bread flour	4 cups white bread flour
1⅓ teaspoons bread machine or instant yeast	2 teaspoons bread machine or instant yeast	2½ teaspoons bread machine or instant yeast

1. Place the ingredients in your bread machine as recommended by the manufacturer.
2. Program the machine for Basic/White bread, select light or medium crust, and press Start.
3. When the loaf is done, remove the bucket from the machine.
4. Let the loaf cool for 5 minutes.
5. Gently shake the bucket to remove the loaf, and turn it out onto a rack to cool.

Ingredient tip: Making candied ginger at home is quite easy and requires very few ingredients or tools. Simply blanch peeled slices of ginger until they are tender, and then simmer the ginger in a syrup made from sugar in the same weight as the ginger and ¼ cup water. Simmer until the syrup is completely evaporated, and cool the candied ginger on a wire rack.

PER SERVING (1 SLICE): CALORIES: 191; TOTAL FAT: 4G; SATURATED FAT: 2G; CARBOHYDRATES: 32G; FIBER: 2G; SODIUM: 137MG; PROTEIN: 5G

GRAIN, SEED, AND NUT BREADS

Whole-Wheat Seed Bread

PREP TIME IS 10 MINUTES OR LESS

The two seeds in this bread add different attributes, so use both to maintain the delicious balance. Sunflower seeds provide a pleasing, nubby texture without making it difficult to cut the bread. The sesame seeds are fragrant and nutty tasting. This bread makes an excellent peanut butter and banana sandwich for any picky eaters in your family.

8 SLICES / 1 POUND	12 SLICES / 1½ POUNDS	16 SLICES / 2 POUNDS
¾ cup water, at 80°F to 90°F	1⅛ cups water, at 80°F to 90°F	1½ cup water, at 80°F to 90°F
1 tablespoon honey	1½ tablespoons honey	2 tablespoons honey
1 tablespoon melted butter, cooled	1½ tablespoons melted butter, cooled	2 tablespoons melted butter, cooled
½ teaspoon salt	¾ teaspoon salt	1 teaspoon salt
2 cups whole-wheat flour	2½ cups whole-wheat flour	3 cups whole-wheat flour
½ cup white bread flour	¾ cup white bread flour	1 cup white bread flour
2 tablespoons raw sunflower seeds	3 tablespoons raw sunflower seeds	¼ cup raw sunflower seeds
1 tablespoon sesame seeds	1 tablespoon sesame seeds	2 tablespoons sesame seeds
1 teaspoon bread machine or instant yeast	1½ teaspoons bread machine or instant yeast	2¼ teaspoons bread machine yeast or instant yeast

1. Place the ingredients in your bread machine as recommended by the manufacturer.
2. Program the machine for Whole-Wheat/Whole-Grain bread, select light or medium crust, and press Start.
3. When the loaf is done, remove the bucket from the machine.
4. Let the loaf cool for 5 minutes.
5. Gently shake the bucket to remove the loaf, and turn it out onto a rack to cool.

Substitution tip: Flaxseed and pumpkin seeds can be used in this rustic bread if you prefer their flavor or have them in the pantry. Whenever possible, keep the sesame seeds as an ingredient because their rich flavor is exceptional.

PER SERVING (1 SLICE): CALORIES: 157; TOTAL FAT: 3G; SATURATED FAT: 1G; CARBOHYDRATES: 29G; FIBER: 1G; SODIUM: 159MG; PROTEIN: 4G

Multigrain Bread

PREP TIME IS 10 MINUTES OR LESS

Multigrain flours can contain a range of different types of grains depending on the brand. Some common additions are rye, triticale, oats, barley, brown rice, millet, flax-seed, and corn. This type of flour also contains whole-wheat flour with all parts of the wheat berry as a base.

8 SLICES / 1 POUND

¾ cups water,
at 80°F to 90°F

1 tablespoon melted
butter, cooled

½ tablespoon honey

½ teaspoon salt

¾ cup multigrain flour

1⅓ cups white bread flour

1 teaspoon bread machine
or active dry yeast

12 SLICES / 1½ POUNDS

1 cup plus 2 tablespoons
water, at 80°F to 90°F

2 tablespoons melted
butter, cooled

1½ tablespoons honey

1½ teaspoons salt

1 cup plus 2 tablespoons
multigrain flour

2 cups white bread flour

1½ teaspoons bread
machine or active dry yeast

16 SLICES / 2 POUNDS

1½ cups water,
at 80°F to 90°F

2 tablespoons melted
butter, cooled

1 tablespoon honey

1 teaspoon salt

1½ cups multigrain flour

2¾ cups white bread flour

2 teaspoons bread machine
or active dry yeast

1. Place the ingredients in your bread machine as recommended by the manufacturer.

2. Program the machine for Basic/White bread, select light or medium crust, and press Start.

3. When the loaf is done, remove the bucket from the machine.

4. Let the loaf cool for 5 minutes.

5. Gently shake the bucket to remove the loaf, and turn it out onto a rack to cool.

Substitution tip: Whole-grain cereals can be substituted for specialty flours such as Bob's Red Mill®. These cereals make your bread denser and very flavorful.

PER SERVING (1 SLICE): CALORIES: 145; TOTAL FAT: 2G; SATURATED FAT: 1G; CARBOHYDRATES: 27G; FIBER: 1G; SODIUM: 305MG; PROTEIN: 4G

Toasted Pecan Bread

PREP TIME IS 10 MINUTES OR LESS

When you bite into a warm slice of this freshly baked bread, it will instantly fill your heart and tummy with cozy comfort. This tender, nut-studded loaf is delicious with a little cinnamon butter or a spoon of honey. Toasting the nuts is crucial to create the rich flavor.

8 SLICES / 1 POUND	12 SLICES / 1 ½ POUNDS	16 SLICES / 2 POUNDS
⅔ cup milk, at 70°F to 80°F	1 cup milk, at 70°F to 80°F	1 ⅓ cup milk, at 70°F to 80°F
4 teaspoons melted butter, cooled	2 tablespoons melted butter, cooled	2 ⅔ tablespoons melted butter, cooled
1 egg, at room temperature	1 egg, at room temperature	1 egg, at room temperature
4 teaspoons sugar	2 tablespoons sugar	2 ⅔ tablespoons sugar
⅔ teaspoon salt	1 teaspoon salt	1 ⅓ teaspoons salt
2 cups white bread flour	3 cups white bread flour	4 cups white bread flour
1 teaspoon bread machine or instant yeast	1 ½ teaspoons bread machine or instant yeast	2 teaspoons bread machine or instant yeast
⅔ cup chopped pecans, toasted	1 cup chopped pecans, toasted	1 ⅓ cups chopped pecans, toasted

1. Place the ingredients, except the pecans, in your bread machine as recommended by the manufacturer.
2. Program the machine for Basic/White bread, select light or medium crust, and press Start.
3. When the machine signals, add the pecans, or put them in a nut/raisin hopper and the machine will add them automatically.
4. When the loaf is done, remove the bucket from the machine.
5. Let the loaf cool for 5 minutes.
6. Gently shake the bucket to remove the loaf, and turn it out onto a rack to cool.

"Did You Know?" More than 80 percent of the world's pecan crop is supplied by the United States. In Albany, Georgia, the pecan capital of the world, there are more than 600,000 pecan trees. Pecan trees can live at least 200 years and produce nuts every two years.

PER SERVING (1 SLICE): CALORIES: 172; TOTAL FAT: 5G; SATURATED FAT: 2G; CARBOHYDRATES: 27G; FIBER: 2G; SODIUM: 224MG; PROTEIN: 5G

Market Seed Bread

PREP TIME IS 10 MINUTES OR LESS

The texture of this bread is hearty enough for any sandwich filling, but the addition of sesame seeds creates an almost delicate flavor. For a truly spectacular result, use toasted sesame seeds instead. You can toast them yourself in a nonstick pan placed over low heat for about 5 minutes.

8 SLICES / 1 POUND	12 SLICES / 1½ POUNDS	16 SLICES / 2 POUNDS
¾ cup milk, at 80°F to 90°F	1 cup plus 2 tablespoons milk, at 80°F to 90°F	1½ cups milk, at 80°F to 90°F
1 tablespoon melted butter, cooled	1½ tablespoons melted butter, cooled	2 tablespoons melted butter, cooled
1 tablespoon honey	1½ tablespoons honey	2 tablespoons honey
½ teaspoon salt	¾ teaspoon salt	1 teaspoon salt
2 tablespoons flaxseed	3 tablespoons flaxseed	¼ cup flaxseed
2 tablespoons sesame seeds	3 tablespoons sesame seeds	¼ cup sesame seeds
1 tablespoon poppy seeds	1½ tablespoons poppy seeds	2 tablespoons poppy seeds
¾ cup whole-wheat flour	1¼ cups whole-wheat flour	1½ cups whole-wheat flour
1¼ cups white bread flour	1¾ cups white bread flour	2½ cups white bread flour
1¼ teaspoons bread machine or instant yeast	1¾ teaspoons bread machine or instant yeast	2¼ teaspoons bread machine or instant yeast

1. Place the ingredients in your bread machine as recommended by the manufacturer.
2. Program the machine for Basic/White bread, select light or medium crust, and press Start.
3. When the loaf is done, remove the bucket from the machine.
4. Let the loaf cool for 5 minutes.
5. Gently shake the bucket to remove the loaf, and turn it out onto a rack to cool.

Ingredient tip: Flaxseed is available in both brown and golden varieties in most bulk stores or the baking section of supermarkets. Both varieties will work well in this recipe, and they are an excellent source of the healthful omega-3 fatty acid, alpha-linolenic acid.

~~~~~~

PER SERVING (1 SLICE): CALORIES: 176; TOTAL FAT: 4G; SATURATED FAT: 2G; CARBOHYDRATES: 29G; FIBER: 2G; SODIUM: 170MG; PROTEIN: 5G

Cracked Wheat Bread

PREP TIME IS 10 MINUTES OR LESS

If you enjoy bread with crunchy bits or texture, this is the bread for you. Soaking the cracked wheat softens the bread, but the grains are still very evident in the finished product. If you want a slightly more tender result, swap out the water for milk.

8 SLICES / 1 POUND	12 SLICES / 1½ POUNDS	16 SLICES / 2 POUNDS
2 tablespoons plus 2 teaspoons cracked wheat	¼ cup cracked wheat	¼ cup plus 4 teaspoons cracked wheat
¾ cup plus 4 teaspoons boiling water	1¼ cups boiling water	1⅔ cups boiling water
2⅔ tablespoons melted butter, cooled	¼ cup melted butter, cooled	¼ cup plus 4 teaspoons melted butter, cooled
2 tablespoons honey	3 tablespoons honey	¼ cup honey
1 teaspoon salt	1½ teaspoons salt	2 teaspoons salt
⅔ cup whole-wheat flour	1 cup whole-wheat flour	1⅓ cups whole-wheat flour
1⅓ cups white bread flour	2 cups white bread flour	2⅔ cups white bread flour
1⅓ teaspoons bread machine or instant yeast	2 teaspoons bread machine or instant yeast	2½ teaspoons bread machine or instant yeast

1. Place the cracked wheat and water in the bucket of your bread machine for 30 minutes or until the liquid is 80°F to 90°F.
2. Place the remaining ingredients in your bread machine as recommended by the manufacturer.
3. Program the machine for Basic/White bread, select light or medium crust, and press Start.
4. When the loaf is done, remove the bucket from the machine.
5. Let the loaf cool for 5 minutes.
6. Gently shake the bucket to remove the loaf, and turn it out onto a rack to cool.

"Did You Know?" Cracked wheat is exactly what it sounds like—wheat berries that have been cracked into smaller pieces. Cracked wheat is incredibly nutritious and can help reduce your risk of cardiovascular disease, diabetes, and several types of cancer.

PER SERVING (1 SLICE): CALORIES: 176; TOTAL FAT: 4G; SATURATED FAT: 3G; CARBOHYDRATES: 31G; FIBER: 2G; SODIUM: 310MG; PROTEIN: 4G

Double Coconut Bread

PREP TIME IS 10 MINUTES OR LESS

Coconut is a popular ingredient in many different recipes because it is a great source of concentrated nutrition. Coconut lends itself well to bread because it can be used in both wet and dry ingredients. For an even more intense coconut flavor in your bread, toast the shredded coconut before adding it to the recipe.

8 SLICES / 1 POUND	12 SLICES / 1 ½ POUNDS	16 SLICES / 2 POUNDS
⅔ cup milk, at 80°F to 90°F	1 cup milk, at 80°F to 90°F	1 ⅓ cup milk, at 80°F to 90°F
1 egg, at room temperature	1 egg, at room temperature	1 egg, at room temperature
1 tablespoon melted butter, cooled	1 ½ tablespoons melted butter, cooled	2 tablespoons melted butter, cooled
1 ⅓ teaspoons pure coconut extract	2 teaspoons pure coconut extract	2 ⅔ teaspoons pure coconut extract
1 ⅔ tablespoons sugar	2 ½ tablespoons sugar	3 ⅓ tablespoons sugar
½ teaspoon salt	¾ teaspoon salt	1 teaspoon salt
⅓ cup sweetened shredded coconut	½ cup sweetened shredded coconut	⅔ cup sweetened shredded coconut
2 cups white bread flour	3 cups white bread flour	4 cups white bread flour
1 teaspoon bread machine or instant yeast	1 ½ teaspoons bread machine or instant yeast	2 teaspoons bread machine or instant yeast

1. Place the ingredients in your bread machine as recommended by the manufacturer.
2. Program the machine for Sweet bread, select light or medium crust, and press Start.
3. When the loaf is done, remove the bucket from the machine.
4. Let the loaf cool for 5 minutes.
5. Gently shake the bucket to remove the loaf, and turn it out onto a rack to cool.

Substitution tip: Coconut milk in the carton (not the can) can be used instead of regular milk to intensify the coconut flavor of this bread. If you want the bread to be less sweet, swap the sweetened coconut for the unsweetened variety.

PER SERVING (1 SLICE): CALORIES: 165; TOTAL FAT: 4G; SATURATED FAT: 2G; CARBOHYDRATES: 28G; FIBER: 2G; SODIUM: 175MG; PROTEIN: 5G

Honeyed Bulgur Bread

Bulgur has a rich, nutty flavor. It contains a whole lot of fiber, and delivers a decent amount of protein. Look for 100 percent whole-grain bulgur when buying this product in the store because cracked wheat is sometimes labeled as bulgur incorrectly.

8 SLICES / 1 POUND	12 SLICES / 1½ POUNDS	16 SLICES / 2 POUNDS
½ cup boiling water	¾ cup boiling water	1 cup boiling water
2 tablespoons bulgur wheat	3 tablespoons bulgur wheat	¼ cup bulgur wheat
2 tablespoons quick oats	3 tablespoons quick oats	¼ cup quick oats
1 egg, at room temperature	2 eggs, at room temperature	2 eggs, at room temperature
1 tablespoon melted butter, cooled	1½ tablespoons melted butter, cooled	2 tablespoons melted butter, cooled
1½ tablespoons honey	2¼ tablespoons honey	3 tablespoons honey
¾ teaspoon salt	1 teaspoon salt	1¼ teaspoons salt
1½ cups white bread flour	2¼ cups white bread flour	3 cups white bread flour
1 teaspoon bread machine or instant yeast	1½ teaspoons bread machine or instant yeast	2 teaspoons bread machine or instant yeast

1. Place the water, bulgur, and oats in the bucket of your bread machine for 30 minutes or until the liquid is 80°F to 90°F.
2. Place the remaining ingredients in your bread machine as recommended by the manufacturer.
3. Program the machine for Basic/White bread, select light or medium crust, and press Start.
4. When the loaf is done, remove the bucket from the machine.
5. Let the loaf cool for 5 minutes.
6. Gently shake the bucket to remove the loaf, and turn it out onto a rack to cool.

Cooking tip: It is very important to follow the soaking step for the bulgur or you will end up with very hard pieces of grain scattered throughout your bread. If you'd like, you can soak the bulgur ahead of time, drain it, and add it to the correct temperature water when you want to bake this bread.

PER SERVING (1 SLICE): CALORIES: 136; TOTAL FAT: 3G; SATURATED FAT: 1G; CARBOHYDRATES: 24G; FIBER: 1G; SODIUM: 217MG; PROTEIN: 4G

Flaxseed Honey Bread

PREP TIME IS 10 MINUTES OR LESS

This is a recipe that requires very few ingredients but packs a big flavor. Honey adds sweet overtones to this simple but delicious bread. Ordinary sandwiches made with deli meat or peanut butter and jam become extraordinary when made with a couple of slices from this loaf.

8 SLICES / 1 POUND	12 SLICES / 1½ POUNDS	16 SLICES / 2 POUNDS
¾ cup milk, at 80°F to 90°F	1⅛ cups milk, at 80°F to 90°F	1½ cups water, at 80°F to 90°F
1 tablespoon melted butter, cooled	1½ tablespoons melted butter, cooled	2 tablespoons melted butter, cooled
1 tablespoon honey	1½ tablespoons honey	2 tablespoons honey
¾ teaspoon salt	1 teaspoon salt	2 teaspoons salt
2 tablespoons flaxseed	¼ cup flaxseed	½ cup flaxseed
2 cups white bread flour	3 cups white bread flour	4 cups white bread flour
¾ teaspoon bread machine or instant yeast	1¼ teaspoons bread machine or instant yeast	1½ teaspoons bread machine or instant yeast

1. Place the ingredients in your bread machine as recommended by the manufacturer.
2. Program the machine for Basic/White bread, select light or medium crust, and press Start.
3. When the loaf is done, remove the bucket from the machine.
4. Let the loaf cool for 5 minutes.
5. Gently shake the bucket to remove the loaf, and turn it out onto a rack to cool.

Substitution tip: You can easily swap the melted butter for olive oil or another vegetable oil in this bread recipe. Use the same amount for the best results.

PER SERVING (1 SLICE): CALORIES: 158; TOTAL FAT: 3G; SATURATED FAT: 1G; CARBOHYDRATES: 28G; FIBER: 2G; SODIUM: 215MG; PROTEIN: 6G

Chia Sesame Bread

PREP TIME IS 10 MINUTES OR LESS

The inclusion of chia and sesame seeds in this loaf ensures that it is packed with protein and great for an energy boost. There are just over 5 grams of protein in each slice. The chia seeds are not noticeable from a flavor perspective, because they are ground up, but the sesame seeds have a distinctive taste.

8 SLICES / 1 POUND	12 SLICES / 1½ POUNDS	16 SLICES / 2 POUNDS
¾ cup water, at 80°F to 90°F	1 cup plus 2 tablespoons water, at 80°F to 90°F	1½ cups water, at 80°F to 90°F
1 tablespoon melted butter, cooled	1½ tablespoons melted butter, cooled	2 tablespoons melted butter, cooled
1 tablespoon sugar	1½ tablespoons sugar	2 tablespoons sugar
¾ teaspoon salt	1⅛ teaspoons salt	1½ teaspoons salt
⅓ cup ground chia seeds	½ cup ground chia seeds	¾ cup ground chia seeds
1 tablespoon sesame seeds	1½ tablespoons sesame seeds	2 tablespoons sesame seeds
1⅔ cups white bread flour	2½ cups white bread flour	3¼ cups white bread flour
1 teaspoon bread machine or instant yeast	1½ teaspoons bread machine or instant yeast	2 teaspoons bread machine or instant yeast

1. Place the ingredients in your bread machine as recommended by the manufacturer.
2. Program the machine for Basic/White bread, select light or medium crust, and press Start.
3. When the loaf is done, remove the bucket from the machine.
4. Let the loaf cool for 5 minutes.
5. Gently shake the bucket to remove the loaf, and turn it out onto a rack to cool.

Cooking tip: You can purchase chia seeds already ground up, but it is quite simple to make your own. Simply place the chia seeds in a blender and pulse until they are powdery.

PER SERVING (1 SLICE): CALORIES: 161; TOTAL FAT: 2G; SATURATED FAT: 1G; CARBOHYDRATES: 25G; FIBER: 4G; SODIUM: 205MG; PROTEIN: 5G

Quinoa Whole-Wheat Bread

PREP TIME IS 10 MINUTES OR LESS

Cooked quinoa creates a moist loaf with a hint of nuttiness. The whole-wheat flour ensures a nice dense texture, which supports the grains beautifully. Try this bread with a generous scoop of salmon salad and shredded kale for a special lunch.

8 SLICES / 1 POUND	12 SLICES / 1 ½ POUNDS	16 SLICES / 2 POUNDS
⅔ cup milk, at 80°F to 90°F	1 cup milk, at 80°F to 90°F	1⅓ cup milk, at 80°F to 90°F
½ cup cooked quinoa, cooled	⅔ cup cooked quinoa, cooled	¾ cup cooked quinoa, cooled
2⅔ tablespoons melted butter, cooled	¼ cup melted butter, cooled	5 tablespoons melted butter, cooled
2 teaspoons sugar	1 tablespoon sugar	4 teaspoons sugar
⅔ teaspoon salt	1 teaspoon salt	1⅓ teaspoons salt
2⅔ tablespoons quick oats	¼ cup quick oats	5 tablespoons quick oats
½ cup whole-wheat flour	¾ cup whole-wheat flour	1 cup whole-wheat flour
1 cup white bread flour	1 ½ cups white bread flour	2 cups white bread flour
1 teaspoon bread machine or instant yeast	1 ½ teaspoons bread machine or instant yeast	2 teaspoons bread machine or instant yeast

1. Place the ingredients in your bread machine as recommended by the manufacturer.
2. Program the machine for Basic/White bread, select light or medium crust, and press Start.
3. When the loaf is done, remove the bucket from the machine.
4. Let the loaf cool for 5 minutes.
5. Gently shake the bucket to remove the loaf, and turn it out onto a rack to cool.

"Did You Know?" Most recipes call for rinsing quinoa for a few minutes before cooking to wash away its natural coating, saponin, which may taste bitter to some people. Rinse your quinoa well in cold water according to the instructions on the package. Some boxed quinoa is already prerinsed.

~~~~~~~~~~~~~~~~~~~~~~~~~

PER SERVING (1 SLICE): CALORIES: 158; TOTAL FAT: 5G; SATURATED FAT: 3G; CARBOHYDRATES: 24G; FIBER: 1G; SODIUM: 232MG; PROTEIN: 4G

Peanut Butter Bread

PREP TIME IS 10 MINUTES OR LESS

Peanut lovers will find an excuse to make this bread again and again for snacking and delicious sandwiches. The texture of this loaf is also light enough for toast. If you have leftovers, you can freeze this bread up to 2 months if it is wrapped well in plastic.

12 TO 16 SLICES / 1½ TO 2 POUNDS

1 cup peanut butter

1 cup milk, at 70°F to 80°F

½ cup packed light brown sugar

¼ cup sugar

¼ cup (½ stick) butter, at room temperature

1 egg, at room temperature

2 teaspoons pure vanilla extract

2 cups all-purpose flour

1 tablespoon baking powder

½ teaspoon salt

1. Place the peanut butter, milk, brown sugar, sugar, butter, egg, and vanilla in your bread machine.

2. Program the machine for Quick/Rapid bread and press Start.

3. While the wet ingredients are mixing, stir together the flour, baking powder, and salt in a small bowl.

4. After the first fast mixing is done and the machine signals, add the dry ingredients.

5. When the loaf is done, remove the bucket from the machine.

6. Let the loaf cool for 5 minutes.

7. Gently shake the bucket to remove the loaf, and turn it out onto a rack to cool.

Variation tip: Almond butter, hazelnut butter, and cashew butter are all good alternatives to peanut butter. If you use natural nut butters, stir them thoroughly to disperse the oils that can accumulate on the top of the spread.

PER SERVING (1 SLICE): CALORIES: 294; TOTAL FAT: 16G; SATURATED FAT: 5G; CARBOHYDRATES: 32G; FIBER: 2G; SODIUM: 242MG; PROTEIN: 9G

Toasted Hazelnut Bread

PREP TIME IS 10 MINUTES OR LESS

Nut breads have a European flair because many pastries and dessert breads in Europe feature different types of nuts. Hazelnuts have an even longer history in China and the Black Sea region, including Turkey. The hazelnuts you buy in the supermarket probably came from Turkey because this country is the largest exporter and producer of these nuts in the world.

8 SLICES / 1 POUND	12 SLICES / 1½ POUNDS	16 SLICES / 2 POUNDS
⅔ cup milk, at 70°F to 80°F	1 cup milk, at 70°F to 80°F	1⅓ cup milk, at 70°F to 80°F
1 egg, at room temperature	1 egg, at room temperature	2 eggs, at room temperature
2½ tablespoons melted butter, cooled	3¾ tablespoons melted butter, cooled	5 tablespoons melted butter, cooled
2 tablespoons honey	3 tablespoons honey	¼ cup honey
½ teaspoon pure vanilla extract	¾ teaspoon pure vanilla extract	1 teaspoon pure vanilla extract
½ teaspoon salt	¾ teaspoon salt	1 teaspoon salt
½ cup finely ground toasted hazelnuts	¾ cup finely ground toasted hazelnuts	1 cup finely ground toasted hazelnuts
2 cups white bread flour	3 cups white bread flour	4 cups white bread flour
1 teaspoon bread machine or instant yeast	1½ teaspoons bread machine or instant yeast	2 teaspoons bread machine or instant yeast

1. Place the ingredients in your bread machine as recommended by the manufacturer.
2. Program the machine for Basic/White bread, select light or medium crust, and press Start.
3. When the loaf is done, remove the bucket from the machine.
4. Let the loaf cool for 5 minutes.
5. Gently shake the bucket to remove the loaf, and turn it out onto a rack to cool.

Cooking tip: Hazelnuts toast in about 15 minutes in an oven preheated to 350°F. Let them cool after they are done, and then rub the nuts between your palms to remove their loose bitter skin.

PER SERVING (1 SLICE): CALORIES: 209; TOTAL FAT: 8G; SATURATED FAT: 3G; CARBOHYDRATES: 30G; FIBER: 1G; SODIUM: 154MG; PROTEIN: 4G

Oatmeal Seed Bread

PREP TIME IS 10 MINUTES OR LESS

If you need a hostess gift for a friend or family member, look no further than this golden beauty. Anyone who thinks bread machines produce inferior bread will have to eat their words when they taste this seed- and nut-studded loaf. You can freeze any extras for up to two months in a sealed plastic bag.

8 SLICES / 1 POUND

¾ cup water, at 80°F to 90°F

2 tablespoons melted butter, cooled

2 tablespoons light brown sugar

1 teaspoon salt

2 tablespoons raw sunflower seeds

2 tablespoons pumpkin seeds

1 tablespoon sesame seeds

½ teaspoon anise seeds

¾ cup quick oats

1½ cups white bread flour

1 teaspoon bread machine or instant yeast

12 SLICES / 1½ POUNDS

1⅛ cups water, at 80°F to 90°F

3 tablespoons melted butter, cooled

3 tablespoons light brown sugar

1½ teaspoons salt

3 tablespoons raw sunflower seeds

3 tablespoons pumpkin seeds

2 tablespoons sesame seeds

1 teaspoon anise seeds

1 cup quick oats

2¼ cups white bread flour

1½ teaspoons bread machine or instant yeast

16 SLICES / 2 POUNDS

1½ cups water, at 80°F to 90°F

¼ cup melted butter, cooled

¼ cup light brown sugar

2 teaspoons salt

¼ cup raw sunflower seeds

¼ cup pumpkin seeds

3 tablespoons sesame seeds

1½ teaspoons anise seeds

1½ cups quick oats

3 cups white bread flour

2 teaspoons bread machine or instant yeast

1. Place the ingredients in your bread machine as recommended by the manufacturer.
2. Program the machine for Basic/White bread, select light or medium crust, and press Start.
3. When the loaf is done, remove the bucket from the machine.
4. Let the loaf cool for 5 minutes.
5. Gently shake the bucket to remove the loaf, and turn it out onto a rack to cool.

"Did You Know?" Anise seeds have a sweet, distinctive licorice flavor that gently infuses this bread, allowing for other flavors to come through, as well. Fresh seeds should be a brilliant olive-green to gray-brown color. They contain a good amount of antioxidant vitamins, such as vitamin C and vitamin A.

PER SERVING (1 SLICE): CALORIES: 172; TOTAL FAT: 6G; SATURATED FAT: 2G; CARBOHYDRATES: 26G; FIBER: 2G; SODIUM: 314MG; PROTEIN: 6G

Nutty Wheat Bread

PREP TIME IS 10 MINUTES OR LESS

Nuts, seeds, and whole-wheat flour make for a fiber-packed loaf that is wonderful paired with salmon salad or used to make sweet cinnamon toast. For an even more tender texture, use milk or buttermilk instead of water in the wet ingredients. This recipe, without added milk, would be perfect for a delayed baking cycle.

8 SLICES / 1 POUND

1 cup water, at 80°F to 90°F

4 teaspoons melted butter, cooled

2 teaspoons sugar

1 teaspoon salt

¾ cup plus 1 tablespoon whole-wheat flour

1⅓ cups white bread flour

1 teaspoon bread machine or instant yeast

4 teaspoons chopped almonds

4 teaspoons chopped pecans

4 teaspoons sunflower seeds

12 SLICES / 1½ POUNDS

1½ cups water, at 80°F to 90°F

2 tablespoons melted butter, cooled

1 tablespoon sugar

1½ teaspoons salt

1¼ cups whole-wheat flour

2 cups white bread flour

1¼ teaspoons bread machine or instant yeast

2 tablespoons chopped almonds

2 tablespoons chopped pecans

2 tablespoons sunflower seeds

16 SLICES / 2 POUNDS

2 cups water, at 80°F to 90°F

2⅔ tablespoons melted butter, cooled

4 teaspoons sugar

2 teaspoons salt

1⅔ cups whole-wheat flour

2⅔ cups white bread flour

1⅔ teaspoons bread machine or instant yeast

2⅔ tablespoons chopped almonds

2⅔ tablespoons chopped pecans

2⅔ tablespoons sunflower seeds

1. Place the ingredients, except the almonds, pecans, and seeds, in your bread machine as recommended by the manufacturer.

2. Program the machine for Basic/White bread, select light or medium crust, and press Start.

3. When the machine signals, add the nuts and seeds, or put them in the nut/raisin hopper and let the machine add them automatically.

4. When the loaf is done, remove the bucket from the machine.

5. Let the loaf cool for 5 minutes.

6. Gently shake the bucket to remove the loaf, and turn it out onto a rack to cool.

Variation tip: Other nuts, such as cashews, pistachios, walnuts, or peanuts, would combine well with the other ingredients in this hearty bread. Use the same amounts as for the pecans and almonds.

PER SERVING (1 SLICE): CALORIES: 154; TOTAL FAT: 3G; SATURATED FAT: 1G; CARBOHYDRATES: 27G; FIBER: 1G; SODIUM: 305MG; PROTEIN: 4G

Sunflower Bread

PREP TIME IS 10 MINUTES OR LESS

Sunflower seeds soften when they are baked into bread, so they add only a little texture to finished loaves. The real impact of sunflower seeds is in the flavor. Raw seeds are best—roasted sunflower seeds become slightly bitter if they are cooked too much during the baking process in your bread machine.

8 SLICES / 1 POUND	12 SLICES / 1½ POUNDS	16 SLICES / 2 POUNDS
⅔ cup water, at 80°F to 90°F	1 cup water, at 80°F to 90°F	1⅓ cups water, at 80°F to 90°F
1 egg, at room temperature	1 egg, at room temperature	2 eggs, at room temperature
2 tablespoons melted butter, cooled	3 tablespoons melted butter, cooled	¼ cup melted butter, cooled
2 tablespoons skim milk powder	3 tablespoons skim milk powder	¼ cup skim milk powder
1 tablespoon honey	1½ tablespoons honey	2 tablespoons honey
1 teaspoon salt	1½ teaspoons salt	2 teaspoons salt
½ cup raw sunflower seeds	¾ cup raw sunflower seeds	1 cup raw sunflower seeds
2 cups white bread flour	3 cups white bread flour	4 cups white bread flour
¾ teaspoon bread machine or instant yeast	1 teaspoon bread machine or instant yeast	1¾ teaspoons bread machine or instant yeast

1. Place the ingredients in your bread machine as recommended by the manufacturer.

2. Program the machine for Basic/White bread, select light or medium crust, and press Start.

3. When the loaf is done, remove the bucket from the machine.

4. Let the loaf cool for 5 minutes.

5. Gently shake the bucket to remove the loaf, and turn it out onto a rack to cool.

"Did You Know?" There are about 800 to 2,000 sunflower seeds per sunflower in as little as 100 days after the flowers are planted. Sunflower seeds ripen quickly because the flowers always face the sun.

PER SERVING (1 SLICE): CALORIES: 178; TOTAL FAT: 5G; SATURATED FAT: 2G; CARBOHYDRATES: 28G; FIBER: 2G; SODIUM: 328MG; PROTEIN: 5G

Raisin Seed Bread

PREP TIME IS 10 MINUTES OR LESS

Sweet raisins provide energy, so take a slice of bread along for before or after a workout and as a pregame snack. You'll get a little dried fruit in almost every bite.

8 SLICES / 1 POUND	12 SLICES / 1 ½ POUNDS	16 SLICES / 2 POUNDS
¾ cup milk, at 80°F to 90°F	1 cup plus 2 tablespoons milk, at 80°F to 90°F	1½ cups milk, at 80°F to 90°F
1 tablespoon melted butter, cooled	1½ tablespoons melted butter, cooled	2 tablespoons melted butter, cooled
1 tablespoon honey	1½ tablespoons honey	2 tablespoons honey
½ teaspoon salt	¾ teaspoon salt	1 teaspoon salt
2 tablespoons flaxseed	3 tablespoons flaxseed	¼ cup flaxseed
2 tablespoons sesame seeds	3 tablespoons sesame seeds	¼ cup sesame seeds
¾ cup whole-wheat flour	1¼ cups whole-wheat flour	1½ cups whole-wheat flour
1¼ cups white bread flour	1¾ cups white bread flour	2½ cups white bread flour
1¼ teaspoons bread machine or instant yeast	1¾ teaspoons bread machine or instant yeast	2¼ teaspoons bread machine or instant yeast
¼ cup raisins	⅓ cup raisins	½ cup raisins

1. Place the ingredients, except the raisins, in your bread machine as recommended by the manufacturer.
2. Program the machine for Basic/White bread, select light or medium crust, and press Start.
3. Add the raisins when your bread machine signals, or place the raisins in the raisin/nut hopper and let the machine add them.
4. When the loaf is done, remove the bucket from the machine.
5. Let the loaf cool for 5 minutes.
6. Gently shake the bucket to remove the loaf, and turn it out onto a rack to cool.

Variation tip: Throw in dried blueberries, chopped dried apple or mango, dried cherries, or currants instead of raisins and enjoy the different results.

PER SERVING (1 SLICE): CALORIES: 182; TOTAL FAT: 4G; SATURATED FAT: 2G; CARBOHYDRATES: 32G; FIBER: 2G; SODIUM: 171MG; PROTEIN: 5G

—Chapter Five—

CHEESE BREADS

Cheesy Chipotle Bread

PREP TIME IS 10 MINUTES OR LESS

If you have never cooked with chipotle chili powder, you will be delighted with the smoky hot taste. This spice is not as hot as cayenne but has much more complexity than regular chili powder. If you want to amp up the Southwestern culinary influence, substitute Monterey Jack cheese for the Cheddar.

8 SLICES / 1 POUND	12 SLICES / 1½ POUNDS	16 SLICES / 2 POUNDS
⅔ cup water, at 80°F to 90°F	1 cup water, at 80°F to 90°F	1¼ cups water, at 80°F to 90°F
1½ tablespoons sugar	2¼ tablespoons sugar	3 tablespoons sugar
1½ tablespoons powdered skim milk	2¼ tablespoons powdered skim milk	3 tablespoons powdered skim milk
¾ teaspoon salt	1 teaspoon salt	1½ teaspoons salt
½ teaspoon chipotle chili powder	¾ teaspoon chipotle chili powder	1 teaspoon chipotle chili powder
2 cups white bread flour	3 cups white bread flour	4 cups white bread flour
½ cup (2 ounces) shredded sharp Cheddar cheese	¾ cup (3 ounces) shredded sharp Cheddar cheese	1 cup (4 ounces) shredded sharp Cheddar cheese
¾ teaspoon bread machine or instant yeast	1 teaspoon bread machine or instant yeast	1¼ teaspoons bread machine or instant yeast

1. Place the ingredients in your bread machine as recommended by the manufacturer.
2. Program the machine for Basic/White bread, select light or medium crust, and press Start.
3. When the loaf is done, remove the bucket from the machine.
4. Let the loaf cool for 5 minutes.
5. Gently shake the bucket to remove the loaf, and turn it out onto a rack to cool.

Decoration tip: When the loaf is still hot from the machine and cooling on the rack, sprinkle an additional ½ cup of shredded cheese on top.

PER SERVING (1 SLICE): CALORIES: 139; TOTAL FAT: 1G; SATURATED FAT: 0G; CARBOHYDRATES: 27G; FIBER: 1G; SODIUM: 245MG; PROTEIN: 6G

Roasted Garlic Asiago Bread

PREP TIME IS 10 MINUTES OR LESS

Making garlic bread for a family dinner or guests can take a bit of preparation when you whip up garlic butter and toast the bread in the oven. Why not serve a couple slices of this garlicky fresh bread instead? If you want to dress it up, brush the bread with a little olive oil and grill it lightly on the barbecue.

8 SLICES / 1 POUND	12 SLICES / 1½ POUNDS	16 SLICES / 2 POUNDS
½ cup plus 1 tablespoon milk, at 70°F to 80°F	¾ cup plus 1 tablespoon milk, at 70°F to 80°F	1 cup plus 1 tablespoon milk, at 70°F to 80°F
2⅔ tablespoons melted butter, cooled	¼ cup melted butter, cooled	5 tablespoons melted butter, cooled
⅔ teaspoon minced garlic	1 teaspoon minced garlic	1⅓ teaspoon minced garlic
4 teaspoons sugar	2 tablespoons sugar	2⅔ tablespoons sugar
⅔ teaspoon salt	1 teaspoon salt	1⅓ teaspoons salt
⅓ cup grated Asiago cheese	½ cup (2 ounces) grated Asiago cheese	⅔ cup (2½ ounces) grated Asiago cheese
1¾ cups plus 1 tablespoon white bread flour	2¾ cups white bread flour	3⅔ cups white bread flour
1 teaspoon bread machine or instant yeast	1½ teaspoons bread machine or instant yeast	2¼ teaspoons bread machine or instant yeast
⅓ cup mashed roasted garlic	½ cup mashed roasted garlic	⅔ cup mashed roasted garlic

1. Place the ingredients, except the roasted garlic, in your bread machine as recommended by the manufacturer.

2. Program the machine for Basic/White bread, select light or medium crust, and press Start.

3. Add the roasted garlic when your machine signals or 5 minutes before the last kneading is done.

4. When the loaf is done, remove the bucket from the machine.

5. Let the loaf cool for 5 minutes.

6. Gently shake the bucket to remove the loaf, and turn it out onto a rack to cool.

Substitution tip: Roasted garlic is worth all the effort needed to make it from scratch, but you can buy it premade in tubes at the grocery store.

PER SERVING (1 SLICE): CALORIES: 180; TOTAL FAT: 6G; SATURATED FAT: 4G; CARBOHYDRATES: 27G; FIBER: 1G; SODIUM: 287MG; PROTEIN: 5G

Cheddar Cheese Basil Bread

PREP TIME IS 10 MINUTES OR LESS

Grilled cheese sandwiches, cheese-topped garlic bread, Welsh rarebit, and cheese fondues are all about bread and melted cheese, so why not put the cheese right in the bread? This recipe ensures there is a taste of Cheddar in every bite. The cheese is added with all the other ingredients, so it blends in rather than baking in chunks.

8 SLICES / 1 POUND	12 SLICES / 1½ POUNDS	16 SLICES / 2 POUNDS
⅔ cup milk, at 80°F to 90°F	1 cup milk, at 80°F to 90°F	1⅓ cup milk, at 80°F to 90°F
2 teaspoons melted butter, cooled	1 tablespoon melted butter, cooled	4 teaspoons melted butter, cooled
2 teaspoons sugar	1 tablespoon sugar	4 teaspoons sugar
⅔ teaspoon dried basil	1 teaspoon dried basil	1¼ teaspoons dried basil
½ cup (2 ounces) shredded sharp Cheddar cheese	¾ cup (3 ounces) shredded sharp Cheddar cheese	1 cup (4 ounces) shredded sharp Cheddar cheese
½ teaspoon salt	¾ teaspoon salt	1 teaspoon salt
2 cups white bread flour	3 cups white bread flour	4 cups white bread flour
1 teaspoon bread machine or active dry yeast	1½ teaspoons bread machine or active dry yeast	2 teaspoons bread machine or active dry yeast

1. Place the ingredients in your bread machine as recommended by the manufacturer.
2. Program the machine for Basic/White bread, select light or medium crust, and press Start.
3. When the loaf is done, remove the bucket from the machine.
4. Let the loaf cool for 5 minutes.
5. Gently shake the bucket to remove the loaf, and turn it out onto a rack to cool.

Ingredient tip: Aged Cheddar is not the same as sharp Cheddar, although aging the cheese gives it a very distinctive flavor. You can substitute Cheddar cheese that has been aged at least 2 years for sharp Cheddar in this bread.

PER SERVING (1 SLICE): CALORIES: 166; TOTAL FAT: 4G; SATURATED FAT: 2G; CARBOHYDRATES: 26G; FIBER: 1G; SODIUM: 209MG; PROTEIN: 6G

Jalapeño Corn Bread

PREP TIME IS 10 MINUTES OR LESS

Cheese and hot chile peppers are evident in each morsel of this delicious loaf that is full of complex flavor. This corn bread will definitely strike the right balance between crumbly and tender. Try a slice slathered with sweet butter or accompanying a hearty bowl of chili.

12 TO 16 SLICES / 1½ TO 2 POUNDS

1 cup buttermilk, at 80°F to 90°F

¼ cup melted butter, cooled

2 eggs, at room temperature

1 jalapeño pepper, chopped

1⅓ cups all-purpose flour

1 cup cornmeal

½ cup (2 ounces) shredded Cheddar cheese

¼ cup sugar

1 tablespoon baking powder

½ teaspoon salt

1. Place the buttermilk, butter, eggs, and jalapeño pepper in your bread machine.

2. Program the machine for Quick/Rapid bread and press Start.

3. While the wet ingredients are mixing, stir together the flour, cornmeal, cheese, sugar, baking powder, and salt in a small bowl.

4. After the first fast mixing is done and the machine signals, add the dry ingredients.

5. When the loaf is done, remove the bucket from the machine.

6. Let the loaf cool for 5 minutes.

7. Gently shake the bucket to remove the loaf, and turn it out onto a rack to cool.

Variation tip: Try using half buttermilk and half creamed corn for the 1 cup of buttermilk amount in the recipe for a moist bread and stronger corn flavor.

PER SERVING (1 SLICE): CALORIES: 167; TOTAL FAT: 6G; SATURATED FAT: 3G; CARBOHYDRATES: 24G; FIBER: 1G; SODIUM: 191MG; PROTEIN: 5G

Olive Cheese Bread

PREP TIME IS 10 MINUTES OR LESS

Antipasto platters can be an attractive addition to a buffet dinner or a casual get-together with friends on a sunny patio. You will not need to top the slices of Olive Cheese Bread with anything before stacking the slices on your platter because the taste is so distinctive. Don't be surprised if your guests want the recipe and finish the entire loaf before your evening is done.

8 SLICES / 1 POUND	12 SLICES / 1½ POUNDS	16 SLICES / 2 POUNDS
⅔ cup milk, at 80°F to 90°F	1 cup milk, at 80°F to 90°F	1⅓ cups milk, at 80°F to 90°F
1 tablespoon melted butter, cooled	1½ tablespoons melted butter, cooled	2 tablespoons melted butter, cooled
⅔ teaspoon minced garlic	1 teaspoon minced garlic	1⅓ teaspoon minced garlic
1 tablespoon sugar	1½ tablespoons sugar	2 tablespoons sugar
⅔ teaspoon salt	1 teaspoon salt	1⅓ teaspoons salt
2 cups white bread flour	3 cups white bread flour	4 cups white bread flour
½ cup (2 ounces) shredded Swiss cheese	¾ cup (3 ounces) shredded Swiss cheese	1 cup (4 ounces) shredded Swiss cheese
¾ teaspoon bread machine or instant yeast	1 teaspoon bread machine or instant yeast	1½ teaspoons bread machine or instant yeast
¼ cup chopped black olives	⅓ cup chopped black olives	½ cup chopped black olives

1. Place the ingredients in your bread machine as recommended by the manufacturer, tossing the flour with the cheese first.
2. Program the machine for Basic/White bread, select light or medium crust, and press Start.
3. When the loaf is done, remove the bucket from the machine.
4. Let the loaf cool for 5 minutes.
5. Gently shake the bucket to remove the loaf, and turn it out onto a rack to cool.

Variation tip: Olives and cheese are a common combination in cooking, so these two ingredients will make delicious, savory bread. Green olives can be used instead of black, and other varieties of cheese would taste delightful, as well.

PER SERVING (1 SLICE): CALORIES: 175; TOTAL FAT: 5G; SATURATED FAT: 3G; CARBOHYDRATES: 27G; FIBER: 1G; SODIUM: 260MG; PROTEIN: 6G

Blue Cheese Onion Bread

PREP TIME IS 10 MINUTES OR LESS

The addition of potato flakes in this predominantly cheesy bread might seem surprising, but the flakes add an incredibly rich texture and flavor to the finished bread. The best blue cheese for this recipe is a firmer type such as Stilton, Roquefort, or Valdeón because they will create small pockets of tangy goodness rather than simply melting into the bread.

8 SLICES / 1 POUND	12 SLICES / 1 ½ POUNDS	16 SLICES / 2 POUNDS
¾ cup plus 1 tablespoon water, at 80°F to 90°F	1 ¼ cup water, at 80°F to 90°F	1 ⅔ cup water, at 80°F to 90°F
1 egg, at room temperature	1 egg, at room temperature	1 egg, at room temperature
2 teaspoons melted butter, cooled	1 tablespoon melted butter, cooled	4 teaspoons melted butter, cooled
3 tablespoons powdered skim milk	¼ cup powdered skim milk	5 tablespoons powdered skim milk
2 teaspoons sugar	1 tablespoon sugar	4 teaspoons sugar
½ teaspoon salt	¾ teaspoon salt	1 teaspoon salt
⅓ cup crumbled blue cheese	½ cup (2 ounces) crumbled blue cheese	⅔ cup (2 ½ ounces) crumbled blue cheese
2 teaspoons dried onion flakes	1 tablespoon dried onion flakes	4 teaspoons dried onion flakes
2 cups white bread flour	3 cups white bread flour	4 cups white bread flour
3 tablespoons instant mashed potato flakes	¼ cup instant mashed potato flakes	5 tablespoons instant mashed potato flakes
¾ teaspoon bread machine or active dry yeast	1 teaspoon bread machine or active dry yeast	1 ¼ teaspoons bread machine or active dry yeast

$\longrightarrow$

1. Place the ingredients in your bread machine as recommended by the manufacturer.
2. Program the machine for Basic/White bread, select light or medium crust, and press Start.
3. When the loaf is done, remove the bucket from the machine.
4. Let the loaf cool for 5 minutes.
5. Gently shake the bucket to remove the loaf, and turn it out onto a rack to cool.

Ingredient tip: If you do decide to use Stilton blue cheese for your bread, make sure you cut the rind off the cheese because it is not edible. If you have any Stilton left, pair it with a slice of bread for a snack.

PER SERVING (1 SLICE): CALORIES: 164; TOTAL FAT: 3G; SATURATED FAT: 2G; CARBOHYDRATES: 27G; FIBER: 1G; SODIUM: 250MG; PROTEIN: 6G

Double Cheese Bread

PREP TIME IS 10 MINUTES OR LESS

Cheese bread is a decadent treat for those who like their indulgences savory rather than sweet. Try a slice of this bread with apple butter or peanut butter for a hearty snack.

8 SLICES / 1 POUND	12 SLICES / 1 ½ POUNDS	16 SLICES / 2 POUNDS
¾ cup plus 1 tablespoon milk, at 80°F to 90°F	1 ¼ cups milk, at 80°F to 90°F	1 ⅔ cups milk, at 80°F to 90°F
2 teaspoons butter, melted and cooled	1 tablespoon butter, melted and cooled	4 teaspoons butter, melted and cooled
4 teaspoons sugar	2 tablespoons sugar	2 ⅔ tablespoons sugar
⅔ teaspoon salt	1 teaspoon salt	1 ⅓ teaspoons salt
⅓ teaspoon freshly ground black pepper	½ teaspoon freshly ground black pepper	⅔ teaspoon freshly ground black pepper
Pinch cayenne pepper	Pinch cayenne pepper	Pinch cayenne pepper
1 cup (4 ounces) shredded aged sharp Cheddar cheese	1 ½ cups (6 ounces) shredded aged sharp Cheddar cheese	2 cups (8 ounces) shredded aged sharp Cheddar
⅓ cup shredded or grated Parmesan cheese	½ cup (2 ounces) shredded or grated Parmesan cheese	⅔ cup (2 ½ ounces) shredded or grated Parmesan cheese
2 cups white bread flour	3 cups white bread flour	4 cups white bread flour
¾ teaspoon bread machine or instant yeast	1 ¼ teaspoons bread machine or instant yeast	1 ⅔ teaspoons bread machine or instant yeast

1. Place the ingredients in your bread machine as recommended by the manufacturer.
2. Program the machine for Basic/White bread, select light or medium crust, and press Start.
3. When the loaf is done, remove the bucket from the machine.
4. Let the loaf cool for 5 minutes.
5. Gently shake the bucket to remove the loaf, and turn it out onto a rack to cool.

Variation tip: If you want pockets of melted cheese instead of uniformly distributed cheese, dice the Cheddar into ½-inch chunks instead.

PER SERVING (1 SLICE): CALORIES: 183; TOTAL FAT: 4G; SATURATED FAT: 2G; CARBOHYDRATES: 28G; FIBER: 1G; SODIUM: 344MG; PROTEIN: 9G

Mozzarella and Salami Bread

PREP TIME IS 10 MINUTES OR LESS

Salami adds a spiciness and texture to this cheesy loaf, creating an almost pizza-like treat. Whenever possible, use a drier salami that has been aged longer, so the oil in the meat will not affect your bread composition.

8 SLICES / 1 POUND	12 SLICES / 1 ½ POUNDS	16 SLICES / 2 POUNDS
¾ cup water, at 80°F to 90°F	1 cup water plus 2 tablespoons, at 80°F to 90°F	1½ cups water, at 80°F to 90°F
⅓ cup shredded mozzarella cheese	½ cup (2 ounces) shredded mozzarella cheese	⅔ cup (2½ ounces) shredded mozzarella cheese
4 teaspoons sugar	2 tablespoons sugar	2⅔ tablespoons sugar
⅔ teaspoon salt	1 teaspoon salt	1⅓ teaspoons salt
⅔ teaspoon dried basil	1 teaspoon dried basil	1⅓ teaspoons dried basil
Pinch garlic powder	¼ teaspoon garlic powder	⅓ teaspoon garlic powder
2 cups plus 2 tablespoons white bread flour	3¼ cups white bread flour	4⅓ cups white bread flour
1 teaspoon bread machine or instant yeast	1½ teaspoons bread machine or instant yeast	2 teaspoons bread machine or instant yeast
½ cup finely diced hot German salami	¾ cup finely diced hot German salami	1 cup finely diced hot German salami

1. Place the ingredients, except the salami, in your bread machine as recommended by the manufacturer.
2. Program the machine for Basic/White bread, select light or medium crust, and press Start.
3. Add the salami when your machine signals or 5 minutes before the second kneading cycle is finished.
4. When the loaf is done, remove the bucket from the machine.
5. Let the loaf cool for 5 minutes.
6. Gently shake the bucket to remove the loaf, and turn it out onto a rack to cool.

Substitution tip: Try pepperoni, Black Forest ham, summer sausage, or cooked pancetta for different texture and flavor variations of this bread.

PER SERVING (1 SLICE): CALORIES: 164; TOTAL FAT: 3G; SATURATED FAT: 1G; CARBOHYDRATES: 28G; FIBER: 1G; SODIUM: 304MG; PROTEIN: 6G

Simple Cottage Cheese Bread

PREP TIME IS 10 MINUTES OR LESS

Cottage cheese takes the place of milk in this recipe, creating the same tender bread with the added bonus of a little tanginess. You might think you are enjoying a milder sourdough when you eat a slice. This bread freezes well, so make two loaves to use up your container of cottage cheese.

8 SLICES / 1 POUND	12 SLICES / 1 ½ POUNDS	16 SLICES / 2 POUNDS
⅓ cup water, at 80°F to 90°F	½ cup water, at 80°F to 90°F	⅔ cup water, at 80°F to 90°F
½ cup low-fat cottage cheese, at room temperature	¾ cup cottage cheese, at room temperature	1 cup cottage cheese, at room temperature
1 egg, at room temperature	1 egg, at room temperature	1 egg, at room temperature
4 teaspoons butter, melted and cooled	2 tablespoons butter, melted and cooled	2⅔ tablespoons butter, melted and cooled
2 teaspoons sugar	1 tablespoon sugar	4 teaspoons sugar
⅔ teaspoon salt	1 teaspoon salt	1⅓ teaspoons salt
⅛ teaspoon baking soda	¼ teaspoon baking soda	⅓ teaspoon baking soda
2 cups white bread flour	3 cups white bread flour	4 cups white bread flour
1⅓ teaspoons bread machine or instant yeast	2 teaspoons bread machine or instant yeast	2¼ teaspoons bread machine or instant yeast

1. Place the ingredients in your bread machine as recommended by the manufacturer.
2. Program the machine for Basic/White bread, select light or medium crust, and press Start.
3. When the loaf is done, remove the bucket from the machine.
4. Let the loaf cool for 5 minutes.
5. Gently shake the bucket to remove the loaf, and turn it out onto a rack to cool.

"Did You Know?" You can freeze leftover cottage cheese to use in other recipes but not to eat with a spoon. The curds and whey separate when the product is thawed, creating a watery mess, which tastes fine but does not look appealing.

PER SERVING (1 SLICE): CALORIES: 155; TOTAL FAT: 3G; SATURATED FAT: 2G; CARBOHYDRATES: 26G; FIBER: 1G; SODIUM: 299MG; PROTEIN: 6G

Chile Cheese Bacon Bread

PREP TIME IS 10 MINUTES OR LESS

There are a lot of textures and flavors in this loaf, from the smoky bacon to the hot chilies and rich cheese. It is almost a meal in one slice! If you serve it as a party appetizer, it is sure to wow your guests.

8 SLICES / 1 POUND	12 SLICES / 1 ½ POUNDS	16 SLICES / 2 POUNDS
⅓ cup milk, at 80°F to 90°F	½ cup milk, at 80°F to 90°F	⅔ cup milk, at 80°F to 90°F
1 teaspoon melted butter, cooled	1½ teaspoons melted butter, cooled	2 teaspoons melted butter, cooled
1 tablespoon honey	1½ tablespoons honey	2 tablespoons honey
1 teaspoon salt	1½ teaspoons salt	2 teaspoons salt
⅓ cup chopped and drained green chiles	½ cup chopped and drained green chiles	⅔ cup chopped and drained green chiles
⅓ cup grated Cheddar cheese	½ cup (2 ounces) grated Cheddar cheese	⅔ cup (2 ½ ounces) grated Cheddar cheese
⅓ cup chopped cooked bacon	½ cup chopped cooked bacon	⅔ cup chopped cooked bacon
2 cups white bread flour	3 cups white bread flour	4 cups white bread flour
1⅓ teaspoons bread machine or instant yeast	2 teaspoons bread machine or instant yeast	2½ teaspoons bread machine or instant yeast

1. Place the ingredients in your bread machine as recommended by the manufacturer.
2. Program the machine for Basic/White bread, select light or medium crust, and press Start.
3. When the loaf is done, remove the bucket from the machine.
4. Let the loaf cool for 5 minutes.
5. Gently shake the bucket to remove the loaf, and turn it out onto a rack to cool.

"Did You Know?" More than 90 percent of the chiles grown in the world today originate from Mexico. In ancient times, chiles were used as money by Mayan and Inca people, and Aztec women made a paste of this fiery pepper to use as an antiaging treatment for their faces.

PER SERVING (1 SLICE): CALORIES: 174; TOTAL FAT: 4G; SATURATED FAT: 2G; CARBOHYDRATES: 404G; FIBER: 28G; SODIUM: 1MG; PROTEIN: 6G

Italian Parmesan Bread

PREP TIME IS 10 MINUTES OR LESS

If you are a fan of hearty grilled vegetable sandwiches on thick slices of crusty bread, look no further than this loaf. The outside is crusty, and the center has a springy texture. For a real gourmet experience, brush the bread with olive oil and grill it slightly on a low-heat barbecue before assembling the sandwiches. Heaven!

8 SLICES / 1 POUND	12 SLICES / 1 ½ POUNDS	16 SLICES / 2 POUNDS
¾ cup water, at 80°F to 90°F	1 cup plus 2 tablespoons water, at 80°F to 90°F	1½ cups water, at 80°F to 90°F
2 tablespoons melted butter, cooled	3 tablespoons melted butter, cooled	¼ cup melted butter, cooled
2 teaspoons sugar	1 tablespoon sugar	4 teaspoons sugar
⅔ teaspoon salt	1 teaspoon salt	1⅓ teaspoons salt
1⅓ teaspoons chopped fresh basil	2 teaspoons chopped fresh basil	1 tablespoon chopped fresh basil
2⅔ tablespoons grated Parmesan cheese	¼ cup grated Parmesan cheese	⅓ cup grated Parmesan cheese
2⅓ cups white bread flour	3½ cups white bread flour	4½ cups white bread flour
1 teaspoon bread machine or instant yeast	1½ teaspoons bread machine or instant yeast	2 teaspoons bread machine or instant yeast

1. Place the ingredients in your bread machine as recommended by the manufacturer.
2. Program the machine for Basic/White bread, select light or medium crust, and press Start.
3. When the loaf is done, remove the bucket from the machine.
4. Let the loaf cool for 5 minutes.
5. Gently shake the bucket to remove the loaf, and turn it out onto a rack to cool.

Substitution tip: This dry hard cheese from the Parma region of Italy has a distinctive flavor that is hard to replace. You can try Asiago, pecorino romano, or aged provolone cheese if you are in need of a substitute.

PER SERVING (1 SLICE): CALORIES: 171; TOTAL FAT: 4G; SATURATED FAT: 2G; CARBOHYDRATES: 29G; FIBER: 1G; SODIUM: 237MG; PROTEIN: 5G

Rich Cheddar Bread

PREP TIME IS 10 MINUTES OR LESS

Cheddar cheese was initially only available in Somerset, England, although it can be found all over the world today. This cheese is made from cow's milk, and the flavor gets sharper and richer as it ages. Try and find a cheese that is at least two years old for this recipe.

8 SLICES / 1 POUND	12 SLICES / 1 ½ POUNDS	16 SLICES / 2 POUNDS
⅔ cup milk, at 80°F to 90°F	1 cup milk, at 80°F to 90°F	1⅓ cup milk, at 80°F to 90°F
4 teaspoons butter, melted and cooled	2 tablespoons butter, melted and cooled	2⅔ tablespoons butter, melted and cooled
2 tablespoons sugar	3 tablespoons sugar	¼ cup sugar
⅔ teaspoon salt	1 teaspoon salt	1⅓ teaspoons salt
⅓ cup grated aged Cheddar cheese	½ cup (2 ounces) grated aged Cheddar cheese	⅔ cup (2 ½ ounces) grated aged Cheddar cheese
2 cups white bread flour	3 cups white bread flour	4 cups white bread flour
1⅓ teaspoons bread machine or instant yeast	2 teaspoons bread machine or instant yeast	2¼ teaspoons bread machine or instant yeast

1. Place the ingredients in your bread machine as recommended by the manufacturer.
2. Program the machine for Basic/White bread, select light or medium crust, and press Start.
3. When the loaf is done, remove the bucket from the machine.
4. Let the loaf cool for 5 minutes.
5. Gently shake the bucket to remove the loaf, and turn it out onto a rack to cool.

Variation tip: There are many Cheddar varieties on the market in mainstream supermarkets and specialty stores. Applewood-smoked, red wine, chipotle, and horseradish Cheddar cheeses would all be interesting choices to use in making this loaf of bread.

PER SERVING (1 SLICE): CALORIES: 162; TOTAL FAT: 3G; SATURATED FAT: 2G; CARBOHYDRATES: 28G; FIBER: 1G; SODIUM: 247MG; PROTEIN: 5G

Feta Oregano Bread

PREP TIME IS 10 MINUTES OR LESS

Feta cheese produces bread that is slightly salty with a tanginess similar to sourdough bread. If you want little pockets of cheese baked into the bread, reserve half the cheese and add it to the machine about 5 minutes before the second kneading cycle ends. If you don't crumble the feta too small, bigger cheese pieces will remain.

8 SLICES / 1 POUND	12 SLICES / 1½ POUNDS	16 SLICES / 2 POUNDS
⅔ cup milk, at 80°F to 90°F	1 cup milk, at 80°F to 90°F	1⅓ cups milk, at 80°F to 90°F
2 teaspoons melted butter, cooled	1 tablespoon melted butter, cooled	4 teaspoons melted butter, cooled
2 teaspoons sugar	1 tablespoon sugar	4 teaspoons sugar
⅔ teaspoon salt	1 teaspoon salt	1⅓ teaspoons salt
2 teaspoons dried oregano	1 tablespoon dried oregano	4 teaspoons dried oregano
2 cups white bread flour	3 cups white bread flour	4 cups white bread flour
1½ teaspoons bread machine or instant yeast	2¼ teaspoons bread machine or instant yeast	2½ teaspoons bread machine or instant yeast
⅔ cup (2½ ounces) crumbled feta cheese	1 cup (4 ounces) crumbled feta cheese	1⅓ cups (5¼ ounces) crumbled feta cheese

1. Place the ingredients in your bread machine as recommended by the manufacturer.
2. Program the machine for Basic/White bread, select light or medium crust, and press Start.
3. When the loaf is done, remove the bucket from the machine.
4. Let the loaf cool for 5 minutes.
5. Gently shake the bucket to remove the loaf, and turn it out onto a rack to cool.

Substitution tip: You can use fresh oregano in this recipe instead of the dried herb. Use twice as much fresh oregano as dried so the flavor is strong enough to combine well with the feta cheese.

PER SERVING (1 SLICE): CALORIES: 164; TOTAL FAT: 4G; SATURATED FAT: 2G; CARBOHYDRATES: 27G; FIBER: 2G; SODIUM: 316MG; PROTEIN: 6G

Goat Cheese Bread

PREP TIME IS 10 MINUTES OR LESS

Soft and tangy goat cheese, also called chèvre, is the top cheese choice for people who are lactose intolerant because it does not affect the body like cow's milk products. Goats produce milk from March to October, and their cheese is not usually aged more than four months or frozen to ensure a superior quality. If you want to eliminate cow's milk from this recipe, use water instead of milk in the same quantity.

8 SLICES / 1 POUND	12 SLICES / 1 ½ POUNDS	16 SLICES / 2 POUNDS
⅔ cup milk, at 80°F to 90°F	1 cup milk, at 80°F to 90°F	1⅓ cups milk, at 80°F to 90°F
2⅔ tablespoons goat cheese, at room temperature	¼ cup goat cheese, at room temperature	5 tablespoons goat cheese, at room temperature
1 tablespoon honey	1½ tablespoons honey	2 tablespoons honey
⅔ teaspoon salt	1 teaspoon salt	1⅓ teaspoons salt
⅔ teaspoon freshly cracked black pepper	1 teaspoon freshly cracked black pepper	1⅓ teaspoons freshly cracked black pepper
2 cups white bread flour	3 cups white bread flour	4 cups white bread flour
1 teaspoon bread machine or instant yeast	1½ teaspoons bread machine or instant yeast	2 teaspoons bread machine or instant yeast

1. Place the ingredients in your bread machine as recommended by the manufacturer.

2. Program the machine for Basic/White bread, select light or medium crust, and press Start.

3. When the loaf is done, remove the bucket from the machine.

4. Let the loaf cool for 5 minutes.

5. Gently shake the bucket to remove the loaf, and turn it out onto a rack to cool.

Variation tip: Try herbed, chipotle, raspberry, or roasted garlic goat cheese instead of plain in this recipe. Each will impart a slightly different taste to the finished loaf.

PER SERVING (1 SLICE): CALORIES: 145; TOTAL FAT: 2G; SATURATED FAT: 1G; CARBOHYDRATES: 27G; FIBER: 1G; SODIUM: 213MG; PROTEIN: 5G

Mozzarella-Herb Bread

PREP TIME IS 10 MINUTES OR LESS

Mozzarella is an often-underappreciated cheese that is relegated to pizzas in most North American restaurants. This fresh cheese was traditionally made from water buffalo milk and eaten a few hours after it was made, rather than aged. Commercial mozzarella in the supermarket is not true mozzarella, but it still tastes delicious and melts beautifully.

8 SLICES / 1 POUND	12 SLICES / 1½ POUNDS	16 SLICES / 2 POUNDS
¾ cup plus 1 tablespoon milk, at 80°F to 90°F	1¼ cups milk, at 80°F to 90°F	1⅔ cups milk, at 80°F to 90°F
2 teaspoons butter, melted and cooled	1 tablespoon butter, melted and cooled	4 teaspoons butter, melted and cooled
4 teaspoons sugar	2 tablespoons sugar	2⅔ tablespoons sugar
⅔ teaspoon salt	1 teaspoon salt	1⅓ teaspoons salt
1⅓ teaspoons dried basil	2 teaspoons dried basil	2⅔ teaspoons dried basil
⅔ teaspoon dried oregano	1 teaspoon dried oregano	1⅓ teaspoons dried oregano
1 cup (4 ounces) shredded mozzarella cheese	1½ cups (6 ounces) shredded mozzarella cheese	1½ cups (6 ounces) shredded mozzarella cheese
2 cups white bread flour	3 cups white bread flour	4 cups white bread flour
1½ teaspoons bread machine or instant yeast	2¼ teaspoons bread machine or instant yeast	2½ teaspoons bread machine or instant yeast

1. Place the ingredients in your bread machine as recommended by the manufacturer.

2. Program the machine for Basic/White bread, select light or medium crust, and press Start.

3. When the loaf is done, remove the bucket from the machine.

4. Let the loaf cool for 5 minutes.

5. Gently shake the bucket to remove the loaf, and turn it out onto a rack to cool.

Decoration tip: If you are at home, quickly sprinkle about ½ cup shredded mozzarella cheese on the loaf after the last rise cycle in the machine. The cheese will melt and bake into golden strands.

PER SERVING (1 SLICE): CALORIES: 186; TOTAL FAT: 4G; SATURATED FAT: 3G; CARBOHYDRATES: 28G; FIBER: 1G; SODIUM: 300MG; PROTEIN: 8G

—Chapter Six—

FRUIT BREADS

Fragrant Orange Bread

PREP TIME IS 10 MINUTES OR LESS

Orange zest adds an intense citrus flavor and pretty flecks of color to this fragrant bread. You might want to serve it with cream cheese and strawberry jam or thin slices of roasted chicken for a special lunch. This recipe is not appropriate to use with a delayed timer because of the milk.

8 SLICES / 1 POUND	12 SLICES / 1½ POUNDS	16 SLICES / 2 POUNDS
1¼ cups milk, at 80°F to 90°F	1 cup milk, at 80°F to 90°F	1¼ cups milk, at 80°F to 90°F
2 tablespoons freshly squeezed orange juice, at room temperature	3 tablespoons freshly squeezed orange juice, at room temperature	¼ cup freshly squeezed orange juice, at room temperature
2 tablespoons sugar	3 tablespoons sugar	¼ cup sugar
¾ tablespoon melted butter, cooled	1 tablespoon melted butter, cooled	1½ tablespoons melted butter, cooled
¾ teaspoon salt	1 teaspoon salt	1¼ teaspoons salt
2 cups white bread flour	3 cups white bread flour	4 cups white bread flour
Zest of ½ orange	Zest of 1 orange	Zest of 1 orange
1 teaspoon bread machine or instant yeast	1¼ teaspoons bread machine or instant yeast	1¾ teaspoons bread machine or instant yeast

1. Place the ingredients in your bread machine as recommended by the manufacturer.
2. Program the machine for Basic/White bread, select light or medium crust, and press Start.
3. When the loaf is done, remove the bucket from the machine.
4. Let the loaf cool for 5 minutes.
5. Gently shake the bucket to remove the loaf, and turn it out onto a rack to cool.

Cooking tip: Check the dough after it has been mixed and kneaded for 5 to 10 minutes, and make any adjustments that are required. If the dough is too dry, add a tablespoon of water. If it looks too wet, add flour by the teaspoon until the dough is smooth.

PER SERVING (1 SLICE): CALORIES: 147; TOTAL FAT: 2G; SATURATED FAT: 1G; CARBOHYDRATES: 28G; FIBER: 1G; SODIUM: 211MG; PROTEIN: 4G

Moist Oatmeal Apple Bread

PREP TIME IS 10 MINUTES OR LESS

You will want to wait until this tender, moist bread is completely cooled before slicing so the slices keep their shape, but the aroma will tempt you to cut it while it is still warm. This bread tastes wonderful topped with a tablespoon or two of almond butter. Add apple slices to a sandwich made with this bread for even more apple flavor.

8 SLICES / 1 POUND	12 SLICES / 1½ POUNDS	16 SLICES / 2 POUNDS
½ cup milk, at 80°F to 90°F	⅔ cup milk, at 80°F to 90°F	1 cup milk, at 80°F to 90°F
2¾ tablespoons unsweetened applesauce, at room temperature	¼ cup unsweetened applesauce, at room temperature	⅓ cup unsweetened applesauce, at room temperature
2 teaspoons melted butter, cooled	1 tablespoon melted butter, cooled	4 teaspoons melted butter, cooled
2 teaspoons sugar	1 tablespoon sugar	4 teaspoons sugar
⅔ teaspoon salt	1 teaspoon salt	1⅓ teaspoons salt
¼ teaspoon ground cinnamon	½ teaspoon ground cinnamon	¾ teaspoon ground cinnamon
Pinch ground nutmeg	Pinch ground nutmeg	Pinch ground nutmeg
2¾ tablespoons quick oats	¼ cup quick oats	⅓ cup quick oats
1½ cups white bread flour	2¼ cups white bread flour	3 cups white bread flour
1½ teaspoons bread machine or active dry yeast	2¼ teaspoons bread machine or active dry yeast	2¼ teaspoons bread machine or active dry yeast

1. Place the ingredients in your bread machine as recommended by the manufacturer.

2. Program the machine for Basic/White bread, select light or medium crust, and press Start.

3. When the loaf is done, remove the bucket from the machine.

4. Let the loaf cool for 5 minutes.

5. Gently shake the bucket to remove the loaf, and turn it out onto a rack to cool.

Ingredient tip: Homemade applesauce is a healthy choice for baking, but the unsweetened variety is preferred so you don't add too much sugar to the bread recipe.

PER SERVING (1 SLICE): CALORIES: 115; TOTAL FAT: 2G; SATURATED FAT: 1G; CARBOHYDRATES: 22G; FIBER: 1G; SODIUM: 208MG; PROTEIN: 3G

Strawberry Shortcake Bread

PREP TIME IS 10 MINUTES OR LESS

You might be wondering how slices of strawberry remain suspended in the finished bread and don't end up all at the bottom of the loaf. The oats in the recipe create a denser product, which supports the fresh fruit and soaks up any juice from the berries. This bread is not easy to cut perfectly, but it is so delicious that it won't matter.

8 SLICES / 1 POUND	12 SLICES / 1½ POUNDS	16 SLICES / 2 POUNDS
¾ cup milk, at 80°F to 90°F	1⅛ cups milk, at 80°F to 90°F	1½ cups milk, at 80°F to 90°F
2 tablespoons melted butter, cooled	3 tablespoons melted butter, cooled	¼ cup melted butter, cooled
2 tablespoons sugar	3 tablespoons sugar	¼ cup sugar
1 teaspoon salt	1½ teaspoons salt	2 teaspoons salt
½ cup sliced fresh strawberries	¾ cup sliced fresh strawberries	1 cup sliced fresh strawberries
¾ cup quick oats	1 cup quick oats	1½ cups quick oats
1½ cups white bread flour	2¼ cups white bread flour	3 cups white bread flour
1 teaspoon bread machine or instant yeast	1½ teaspoons bread machine or instant yeast	2 teaspoons bread machine or instant yeast

1. Place the ingredients in your bread machine as recommended by the manufacturer.
2. Program the machine for Basic/White bread, select light or medium crust, and press Start.
3. When the loaf is done, remove the bucket from the machine.
4. Let the loaf cool for 5 minutes.
5. Gently shake the bucket to remove the loaf, and turn it out onto a rack to cool.

Decoration tip: Although this is a proper yeast bread rather than a quick bread, a sprinkling of icing sugar over the top would be a lovely addition. Use a fine mesh sieve or a flour sifter to create an even drift of sugar.

PER SERVING (1 SLICE): CALORIES: 162; TOTAL FAT: 4G; SATURATED FAT: 2G; CARBOHYDRATES: 27G; FIBER: 2G; SODIUM: 322MG; PROTEIN: 4G

Pineapple Coconut Bread

PREP TIME IS 10 MINUTES OR LESS

Pineapple juice has an assertive taste that you will really enjoy in this sweet bread. This loaf will make a wonderful dessert to serve to family and friends, or enjoyed with tea or coffee at any time of the day. Toast the coconut before adding it to the recipe if you want to add some rich, nutty flavor.

12 TO 16 SLICES / 1 ½ TO 2 POUNDS

6 tablespoons butter, at room temperature

2 eggs, at room temperature

½ cup coconut milk, at room temperature

½ cup pineapple juice, at room temperature

1 cup sugar

1 ½ teaspoons coconut extract

2 cups all-purpose flour

¾ cup shredded sweetened coconut

1 teaspoon baking powder

½ teaspoon salt

1. Place the butter, eggs, coconut milk, pineapple juice, sugar, and coconut extract in your bread machine.
2. Program the machine for Quick/Rapid bread and press Start.
3. While the wet ingredients are mixing, stir together the flour, coconut, baking powder, and salt in a small bowl.
4. After the first fast mixing is done and the machine signals, add the dry ingredients.
5. When the loaf is done, remove the bucket from the machine.
6. Let the loaf cool for 5 minutes.
7. Gently shake the bucket to remove the loaf, and turn it out onto a rack to cool.

"Did You Know?" It takes about three years for a pineapple to mature enough to be edible, and this sweet fruit does not continue to ripen after it is picked. Once you have cut a pineapple, eat the succulent flesh quickly because it will last less than a week in the refrigerator.

PER SERVING (1 SLICE): CALORIES: 249; TOTAL FAT: 11G; SATURATED FAT: 7G; CARBOHYDRATES: 36G; FIBER: 2G; SODIUM: 153MG; PROTEIN: 3G

Warm Spiced Pumpkin Bread

PREP TIME IS 10 MINUTES OR LESS

Pumpkin is a vegetable that is often prepared like a fruit because its flavor has an affinity for sweeteners and warm spicing. This bread is similar in texture to banana bread with a slightly finer crumb. You can toast and butter it for a delicious, simple breakfast or eat a cold slice on the go for an afternoon energy pick-me-up.

12 TO 16 SLICES / 1½ TO 2 POUNDS

Butter for greasing the bucket

1½ cups pumpkin purée

3 eggs, at room temperature

⅓ cup melted butter, cooled

1 cup sugar

3 cups all-purpose flour

1½ teaspoons baking powder

¾ teaspoon ground cinnamon

½ teaspoon baking soda

¼ teaspoon ground nutmeg

¼ teaspoon ground ginger

¼ teaspoon salt

Pinch ground cloves

1. Lightly grease the bread bucket with butter.

2. Add the pumpkin, eggs, butter, and sugar.

3. Program the machine for Quick/Rapid bread and press Start.

4. Let the wet ingredients be mixed by the paddles until the first fast mixing cycle is finished, about 10 minutes into the cycle.

5. While the wet ingredients are mixing, stir together the flour, baking powder, cinnamon, baking soda, nutmeg, ginger, salt, and cloves until well blended.

6. Add the dry ingredients to the bucket when the second fast mixing cycle starts.

7. Scrape down the sides of the bucket once after the dry ingredients are mixed into the wet.

8. When the loaf is done, remove the bucket from the machine.

9. Let the loaf cool for 5 minutes.

10. Gently shake the bucket to remove the loaf, and turn it out onto a rack to cool.

Substitution tip: Chopped pecans or walnuts can be added to the batter if you enjoy a little crunch in your quick bread.

PER SERVING (1 SLICE): CALORIES: 251; TOTAL FAT: 7G; SATURATED FAT: 4G; CARBOHYDRATES: 43G; FIBER: 2G; SODIUM: 159MG; PROTEIN: 5G

Black Olive Bread

PREP TIME IS 10 MINUTES OR LESS

If you are feeling adventurous when making this bread, add whole pitted olives instead of chopped olives before the second rising. Simply press the olives into the dough so the bread rises around them. This ensures a beautiful appearance when the bread is sliced and prevents the olives from burning while baking.

8 SLICES / 1 POUND

⅔ cup milk, at 80°F to 90°F

1 tablespoon melted butter, cooled

⅔ teaspoon minced garlic

1 tablespoon sugar

⅔ teaspoon salt

2 cups white bread flour

¾ teaspoon bread machine or instant yeast

¼ cup chopped black olives

12 SLICES / 1 ½ POUNDS

1 cup milk, at 80°F to 90°F

1½ tablespoons melted butter, cooled

1 teaspoon minced garlic

1½ tablespoons sugar

1 teaspoon salt

3 cups white bread flour

1 teaspoon bread machine or instant yeast

⅓ cup chopped black olives

16 SLICES / 2 POUNDS

1⅓ cups milk, at 80°F to 90°F

2 tablespoons melted butter, cooled

1⅓ teaspoons minced garlic

2 tablespoons sugar

1⅓ teaspoons salt

4 cups white bread flour

1½ teaspoons bread machine or instant yeast

½ cup chopped black olives

1. Place the ingredients in your bread machine as recommended by the manufacturer.

2. Program the machine for Basic/White bread, select light or medium crust, and press Start.

3. When the loaf is done, remove the bucket from the machine.

4. Let the loaf cool for 5 minutes.

5. Gently shake the bucket to remove the loaf, and turn it out onto a rack to cool.

Machine tip: The olives in this recipe are added along with the rest of the ingredients so they get torn up and dispersed in the bread in little bits. If you want bigger olive chunks, add them when your machine signals or 5 minutes before the last kneading cycle ends.

PER SERVING (1 SLICE): CALORIES: 148; TOTAL FAT: 3G; SATURATED FAT: 1G; CARBOHYDRATES: 27G; FIBER: 1G; SODIUM: 247MG; PROTEIN: 4G

Robust Date Bread

PREP TIME IS 10 MINUTES OR LESS

Imagine thin slices of rare roast beef, Gouda cheese, ripe tomato, piles of crunchy alfalfa sprouts, and a thick slathering of hot mustard. You would need a robust bread to hold all those ingredients together, such as this rustic loaf. The fiber-rich flour and chopped dates create bread with substance and an assertive flavor for toppings that need a little stability.

8 SLICES / 1 POUND	12 SLICES / 1½ POUNDS	16 SLICES / 2 POUNDS
½ cup water, at 80°F to 90°F	¾ cup water, at 80°F to 90°F	1 cup water, at 80°F to 90°F
½ cup milk, at 80°F	½ cup milk, at 80°F	½ cup milk, at 80°F
1½ tablespoons melted butter, cooled	2 tablespoons melted butter, cooled	2 tablespoons melted butter, cooled
3 tablespoons honey	¼ cup honey	5 tablespoons honey
2 tablespoons molasses	3 tablespoons molasses	3 tablespoons molasses
1½ teaspoons sugar	1 tablespoon sugar	1 tablespoon sugar
1 tablespoon skim milk powder	2 tablespoons skim milk powder	3 tablespoons skim milk powder
½ teaspoon salt	1 teaspoon salt	1 teaspoon salt
1½ cups whole-wheat flour	2¼ cups whole-wheat flour	2½ cups whole-wheat flour
1 cup white bread flour	1¼ cups white bread flour	2 cups white bread flour
2 teaspoons unsweetened cocoa powder	1 tablespoon unsweetened cocoa powder	1 tablespoon unsweetened cocoa powder
1 teaspoon bread machine or instant yeast	1½ teaspoons bread machine or instant yeast	1½ teaspoons bread machine or instant yeast
½ cup chopped dates	¾ cup chopped dates	1 cup chopped dates

1. Place the ingredients, except the dates, in your bread machine as recommended by the manufacturer.
2. Program the machine for Basic/White bread, select light or medium crust, and press Start.
3. When the machine signals, add the chopped dates, or put them in the nut/raisin hopper and let the machine add them automatically.
4. When the loaf is done, remove the bucket from the machine.
5. Let the loaf cool for 5 minutes.
6. Gently shake the bucket to remove the loaf, and turn it out onto a rack to cool.

Machine tip: If your machine does not have an "add nut/raisin" signal or hopper, add the dates at the end of the second kneading cycle.

PER SERVING (1 SLICE): CALORIES: 233; TOTAL FAT: 3G; SATURATED FAT: 2G; CARBOHYDRATES: 42G; FIBER: 2G; SODIUM: 223MG; PROTEIN: 5G

Apple Spice Bread

PREP TIME IS 10 MINUTES OR LESS

Adding apple chunks to clove-scented bread is an inspired idea. The type of apple you use can change the taste of the bread, from tart McIntosh apples to sweet Red Delicious apples. You can even experiment and use more than one variety.

8 SLICES / 1 POUND	12 SLICES / 1 ½ POUNDS	16 SLICES / 2 POUNDS
⅔ cup milk, at 80°F to 90°F	1 cup milk, at 80°F to 90°F	1⅓ cup milk, at 80°F to 90°F
1⅔ tablespoons melted butter, cooled	2½ tablespoons melted butter, cooled	3⅓ tablespoons melted butter, cooled
4 teaspoons sugar	2 tablespoons sugar	2⅔ tablespoons sugar
1 teaspoon salt	1½ teaspoons salt	2 teaspoons salt
⅔ teaspoon ground cinnamon	1 teaspoon ground cinnamon	1⅓ teaspoons ground cinnamon
Pinch ground cloves	Pinch ground cloves	Pinch ground cloves
2 cups white bread flour	3 cups white bread flour	4 cups white bread flour
1½ teaspoons bread machine or active dry yeast	2¼ teaspoons bread machine or active dry yeast	2¼ teaspoons bread machine or active dry yeast
⅔ cup finely diced peeled apple	1 cup finely diced peeled apple	1⅓ cups finely diced peeled apple

1. Place the ingredients, except the apple, in your bread machine as recommended by the manufacturer.
2. Program the machine for Basic/White bread, select light or medium crust, and press Start.
3. When the machine signals, add the apple to the bucket, or add it just before the end of the second kneading cycle if your machine does not have a signal.
4. When the loaf is done, remove the bucket from the machine.
5. Let the loaf cool for 5 minutes.
6. Gently shake the bucket to remove the loaf, and turn it out onto a rack to cool.

Variation tip: This recipe is an ideal base for any kind of fruit. Try pears, peaches, nectarines, and any kind of berries in place of the apple.

PER SERVING (1 SLICE): CALORIES: 163; TOTAL FAT: 3G; SATURATED FAT: 2G; CARBOHYDRATES: 29G; FIBER: 2G; SODIUM: 319MG; PROTEIN: 4G

Lemon-Lime Blueberry Bread

PREP TIME IS 10 MINUTES OR LESS

Bread often plays a supporting role in a sandwich or acts as a way to scoop up a flavorful soup or stew. This bread is the one to make if you enjoy bread with a dab of butter or plain. The hint of citrus and sweet-tart blueberries in an almost sourdough-tasting bread is perfect on its own with no embellishments.

8 SLICES / 1 POUND	12 SLICES / 1 ½ POUNDS	16 SLICES / 2 POUNDS
½ cup plain yogurt, at room temperature	¾ cup plain yogurt, at room temperature	1 cup plain yogurt, at room temperature
⅓ cup water, at 80°F to 90°F	½ cup water, at 80°F to 90°F	⅔ cup water, at 80°F to 90°F
2 tablespoons honey	3 tablespoons honey	¼ cup honey
2 teaspoons melted butter, cooled	1 tablespoon melted butter, cooled	4 teaspoons melted butter, cooled
1 teaspoon salt	1 ½ teaspoons salt	2 teaspoons salt
⅓ teaspoon lemon extract	½ teaspoon lemon extract	⅔ teaspoon lemon extract
1 teaspoon lime zest	1 teaspoon lime zest	1 ½ teaspoons lime zest
⅔ cup dried blueberries	1 cup dried blueberries	1 ⅓ cups dried blueberries
2 cups white bread flour	3 cups white bread flour	4 cups white bread flour
1 ½ teaspoons bread machine or instant yeast	2 ¼ teaspoons bread machine or instant yeast	2 ¼ teaspoons bread machine or instant yeast

1. Place the ingredients in your bread machine as recommended by the manufacturer.
2. Program the machine for Basic/White bread, select light or medium crust, and press Start.
3. When the loaf is done, remove the bucket from the machine.
4. Let the loaf cool for 5 minutes.
5. Gently shake the bucket to remove the loaf, and turn it out onto a rack to cool.

Decoration tip: When the bread is cool, slice even pieces and then arrange them on a pretty platter, overlapping, until you have a circle with a space in the middle. Fill the empty center with fresh blueberries and serve as a brunch dish.

PER SERVING (1 SLICE): CALORIES: 159; TOTAL FAT: 2G; SATURATED FAT: 1G; CARBOHYDRATES: 31G; FIBER: 1G; SODIUM: 310MG; PROTEIN: 5G

Banana Whole-Wheat Bread

PREP TIME IS 10 MINUTES OR LESS

This is less of a traditional banana bread than a dense, moist wheat bread with a tantalizing banana flavor. You will want to toast slices and make interesting sandwiches with this bread. Try spicy Thai-influenced chicken with a generous spoon of mango salsa for your first sandwich.

8 SLICES / 1 POUND	12 SLICES / 1 ½ POUNDS	16 SLICES / 2 POUNDS
⅓ cup milk, at 80°F to 90°F	½ cup milk, at 80°F to 90°F	⅔ cup milk, at 80°F to 90°F
⅔ cup mashed banana	1 cup mashed banana	1⅓ cup mashed banana
1 egg, at room temperature	1 egg, at room temperature	1 egg, at room temperature
1 tablespoon melted butter, cooled	1½ tablespoons melted butter, cooled	2 tablespoons melted butter, cooled
2 tablespoons honey	3 tablespoons honey	¼ cup honey
⅔ teaspoon pure vanilla extract	1 teaspoon pure vanilla extract	1⅓ teaspoons pure vanilla extract
⅓ teaspoon salt	½ teaspoon salt	⅔ teaspoon salt
⅔ cup whole-wheat flour	1 cup whole-wheat flour	1⅓ cup whole-wheat flour
¾ cup plus 1 tablespoon white bread flour	1¼ cups white bread flour	1⅔ cups white bread flour
1 teaspoon bread machine or instant yeast	1½ teaspoons bread machine or instant yeast	2 teaspoons bread machine or instant yeast

1. Place the ingredients in your bread machine as recommended by the manufacturer.
2. Program the machine for Sweet bread and press Start.
3. When the loaf is done, remove the bucket from the machine.
4. Let the loaf cool for 5 minutes.
5. Gently shake the bucket to remove the loaf, and turn it out onto a rack to cool.

Cooking tip: If your bananas are not ripe enough for bread, place them in an oven preheated to 250°F for about 15 minutes and then let them cool. They will become sweet and soft with a very black peel you can discard.

PER SERVING (1 SLICE): CALORIES: 145; TOTAL FAT: 2G; SATURATED FAT: 1G; CARBOHYDRATES: 28G; FIBER: 1G; SODIUM: 119MG; PROTEIN: 4G

Orange Cranberry Bread

PREP TIME IS 10 MINUTES OR LESS

The aromatic fragrance of oranges comes from essential oils in its skin, which is why there is a generous amount of zest in this recipe. Scrub the orange well before zesting it to remove any contaminants. You can still eat the orange after zesting off the skin for this bread.

12 TO 16 SLICES / 1½ TO 2 POUNDS

¾ cup milk, at 80°F to 90°F

¾ cup sugar

⅔ cup melted butter, cooled

2 eggs, at room temperature

¼ cup freshly squeezed orange juice, at room temperature

1 tablespoon orange zest

1 teaspoon pure vanilla extract

2¼ cups all-purpose flour

1 cup sweetened dried cranberries

1½ teaspoons baking powder

½ teaspoon baking soda

½ teaspoon salt

¼ teaspoon ground nutmeg

1. Place the milk, sugar, butter, eggs, orange juice, zest, and vanilla in your bread machine.
2. Program the machine for Quick/Rapid bread and press Start.
3. While the wet ingredients are mixing, stir together the flour, cranberries, baking powder, baking soda, salt, and nutmeg in a medium bowl.
4. After the first fast mixing is done and the machine signals, add the dry ingredients.
5. When the loaf is done, remove the bucket from the machine.
6. Let the loaf cool for 5 minutes.
7. Gently shake the bucket to remove the loaf, and turn it out onto a rack to cool.

Machine tip: You can make this bread in a 2-pound machine, but the loaf will not rise as high as if you made it in the 1½-pound bucket. You might also find the finished loaf is a little drier in texture.

PER SERVING (1 SLICE): CALORIES: 206; TOTAL FAT: 7G; SATURATED FAT: 4G; CARBOHYDRATES: 33G; FIBER: 1G; SODIUM: 205MG; PROTEIN: 4G

Plum Orange Bread

PREP TIME IS 10 MINUTES OR LESS

You might be reminded of fruit kuchen the first time you enjoy a slice of this orange-scented bread. Kuchen is a European dessert featuring fruit chunks baked into a plain cake. If you want to re-create this dessert more closely, add a little pure vanilla extract to the wet ingredients.

8 SLICES / 1 POUND

¾ cup water, at 80°F to 90°F

1½ tablespoons melted butter, cooled

2 tablespoons sugar

½ teaspoon salt

½ teaspoon orange zest

¼ teaspoon ground cinnamon

Pinch ground nutmeg

1¼ cups whole-wheat flour

¾ cup white bread flour

1 teaspoon bread machine or instant yeast

¾ cup chopped fresh plums

12 SLICES / 1½ POUNDS

1⅛ cup water, at 80°F to 90°F

2¼ tablespoons melted butter, cooled

3 tablespoons sugar

¾ teaspoon salt

¾ teaspoon orange zest

⅓ teaspoon ground cinnamon

Pinch ground nutmeg

1¾ cups plus 2 tablespoons whole-wheat flour

1⅛ cups white bread flour

1½ teaspoons bread machine or instant yeast

1 cup chopped fresh plums

16 SLICES / 2 POUNDS

1½ cups water, at 80°F to 90°F

3 tablespoons melted butter, cooled

¼ cup sugar

1 teaspoon salt

1 teaspoon orange zest

½ teaspoon ground cinnamon

Pinch ground nutmeg

2½ cups whole-wheat flour

1½ cups white bread flour

2 teaspoons bread machine or instant yeast

1¼ cups chopped fresh plums

1. Place the ingredients, except the plums, in your bread machine as recommended by the manufacturer.
2. Program the machine for Basic/White bread, select light or medium crust, and press Start.
3. When the machine signals, add the chopped plums.
4. When the loaf is done, remove the bucket from the machine.
5. Let the loaf cool for 5 minutes.
6. Gently shake the bucket to remove the loaf, and turn it out onto a rack to cool.

"Did You Know?" There are more than 140 varieties of plums sold in North America, which are mostly Japanese plum hybrids. Inhale the heady fragrance of a ripe plum, and you'll see why this sweet fruit is a member of the rose family.

PER SERVING (1 SLICE): CALORIES: 141; TOTAL FAT: 3G; SATURATED FAT: 1G; CARBOHYDRATES: 26G; FIBER: 1G; SODIUM: 163MG; PROTEIN: 3G

Peaches and Cream Bread

PREP TIME IS 10 MINUTES OR LESS

This recipe uses regular canned peaches packed in light syrup. Even though you are draining the fruit, some of the sugar in the syrup still infuses the peaches. If you are using no-sugar-added canned peaches for the bread, increase the sugar in the recipe by about ½ teaspoon so the ingredients remain balanced.

8 SLICES / 1 POUND	12 SLICES / 1 ½ POUNDS	16 SLICES / 2 POUNDS
½ cup canned peaches, drained and chopped	¾ cup canned peaches, drained and chopped	1 cup canned peaches, drained and chopped
¼ cup heavy whipping cream, at 80°F to 90°F	⅓ cup heavy whipping cream, at 80°F to 90°F	½ cup heavy whipping cream, at 80°F to 90°F
1 egg, at room temperature	1 egg, at room temperature	1 egg, at room temperature
¾ tablespoon melted butter, cooled	1 tablespoon melted butter, cooled	1 ½ tablespoons melted butter, cooled
1 ½ tablespoons sugar	2 ¼ tablespoons sugar	3 tablespoons sugar
¾ teaspoon salt	1 ⅛ teaspoons salt	1 ½ teaspoons salt
¼ teaspoon ground cinnamon	⅓ teaspoon ground cinnamon	½ teaspoon ground cinnamon
⅛ teaspoon ground nutmeg	⅛ teaspoon ground nutmeg	¼ teaspoon ground nutmeg
¼ cup whole-wheat flour	⅓ cup whole-wheat flour	½ cup whole-wheat flour
1 ¾ cups white bread flour	2 ⅔ cups white bread flour	3 ½ cups white bread flour
¾ teaspoons bread machine or instant yeast	1 ⅛ teaspoons bread machine or instant yeast	1 ½ teaspoons bread machine or instant yeast

1. Place the ingredients in your bread machine as recommended by the manufacturer.

2. Program the machine for Basic/White bread, select light or medium crust, and press Start.

3. When the loaf is done, remove the bucket from the machine.

4. Let the loaf cool for 5 minutes.

5. Gently shake the bucket to remove the loaf, and turn it out onto a rack to cool.

Substitution tip: Fresh or frozen peaches can be used as long as they are chopped well and thawed completely. Use the same amount as the canned product, and add it to the wet ingredients.

PER SERVING (1 SLICE): CALORIES: 153; TOTAL FAT: 3G; SATURATED FAT: 2G; CARBOHYDRATES: 27G; FIBER: 1G; SODIUM: 208MG; PROTEIN: 4G

Fresh Blueberry Bread

PREP TIME IS 10 MINUTES OR LESS

You might be reminded of a blueberry muffin when you first bite into this bread. It's soft and moist and just loaded with fresh blueberries. The taste of the bread will change depending on the type of blueberry you add to the recipe: Wild blueberries are tart, and cultivated berries from the grocery store are sweeter.

12 TO 16 SLICES / 1½ TO 2 POUNDS

1 cup plain Greek yogurt, at room temperature

½ cup milk, at room temperature

3 tablespoons butter, at room temperature

2 eggs, at room temperature

½ cup sugar

¼ cup light brown sugar

1 teaspoon pure vanilla extract

½ teaspoon lemon zest

2 cups all-purpose flour

1 tablespoon baking powder

¾ teaspoon salt

¼ teaspoon ground nutmeg

1 cup blueberries

1. Place the yogurt, milk, butter, eggs, sugar, brown sugar, vanilla, and zest in your bread machine.
2. Program the machine for Quick/Rapid bread and press Start.
3. While the wet ingredients are mixing, stir together the flour, baking powder, salt, and nutmeg in a medium bowl.
4. After the first fast mixing is done and the machine signals, add the dry ingredients.
5. When the second mixing cycle is complete, stir in the blueberries.
6. When the loaf is done, remove the bucket from the machine.
7. Let the loaf cool for 5 minutes.
8. Gently shake the bucket to remove the loaf, and turn it out onto a rack to cool.

Ingredient tip: Frozen blueberries will taste very similar to fresh blueberries in this bread, but they will create a blue-tinted loaf rather than a pale quick bread studded with intact fruit. If you don't mind this discoloration, you can make this bread inexpensively year-round and not only when blueberries are in season. Thaw 1 cup frozen blueberries completely, and pat them dry before adding them to the bucket.

PER SERVING (1 SLICE): CALORIES: 185; TOTAL FAT: 4G; SATURATED FAT: 2G; CARBOHYDRATES: 32G; FIBER: 1G; SODIUM: 201MG; PROTEIN: 5G

Blueberry Oatmeal Bread

PREP TIME IS 10 MINUTES OR LESS

With tasty dried blueberries, oatmeal, and honey, this is a wonderful loaf of bread to make on a regular basis. The loaf slices beautifully and is the perfect base for any sandwich filling. This bread also freezes well, so you can always have some on hand.

8 SLICES / 1 POUND	12 SLICES / 1 ½ POUNDS	16 SLICES / 2 POUNDS
⅓ cup milk, at 80°F to 90°F	¾ cup milk, at 80°F to 90°F	1 cup milk, at 80°F to 90°F
1 egg, at room temperature	1 egg, at room temperature	1 egg, at room temperature
1½ tablespoons melted butter, cooled	2¼ tablespoons melted butter, cooled	3 tablespoons melted butter, cooled
1 tablespoon honey	1½ tablespoons honey	2 tablespoons honey
⅓ cup rolled oats	½ cup rolled oats	⅔ cup rolled oats
2 cups white bread flour	2⅓ cups white bread flour	3 cups plus 2 tablespoons white bread flour
¾ teaspoon salt	1⅛ teaspoons salt	1½ teaspoons salt
1 teaspoon bread machine or instant yeast	1½ teaspoons bread machine or instant yeast	2 teaspoons bread machine or instant yeast
⅓ cup dried blueberries	½ cup dried blueberries	⅔ cup dried unsweetened blueberries

1. Place the ingredients, except the blueberries, in your bread machine as recommended by the manufacturer.
2. Program the machine for Basic/White bread, select light or medium crust, and press Start.
3. Add the blueberries when the machine signals or 5 minutes before the second kneading cycle is finished.
4. When the loaf is done, remove the bucket from the machine.
5. Let the loaf cool for 5 minutes.
6. Gently shake the bucket to remove the loaf, and turn it out onto a rack to cool.

Variation tip: Any dried fruit would be delightful in this bread, including cherries, currants, apple, all types of raisins, and cranberries.

PER SERVING (1 SLICE): CALORIES: 147; TOTAL FAT: 3G; SATURATED FAT: 2G; CARBOHYDRATES: 25G; FIBER: 1G; SODIUM: 223MG; PROTEIN: 4G

—Chapter Seven—

VEGETABLE BREADS

Yeasted Carrot Bread

PREP TIME IS 20 MINUTES OR LESS

Most carrot breads are dense dessert–like creations that aren't well suited for making a sandwich or dipping into a thick stew. However, this carrot bread is a real yeast-raised bread with just the right texture and sweetness for a chicken salad sandwich. The tiny orange flecks look pretty no matter how you choose to eat the bread.

8 SLICES / 1 POUND	12 SLICES / 1½ POUNDS	16 SLICES / 2 POUNDS
½ cup milk, at 80°F to 90°F	¾ cup milk, at 80°F to 90°F	1 cup milk, at 80°F to 90°F
2 tablespoons melted butter, cooled	3 tablespoons melted butter, cooled	¼ cup melted butter, cooled
1 tablespoon honey	1 tablespoon honey	1 tablespoon honey
1 cup shredded carrot	1½ cups shredded carrot	2 cups shredded carrot
½ teaspoon ground nutmeg	¾ teaspoon ground nutmeg	1 teaspoon ground nutmeg
¼ teaspoon salt	½ teaspoon salt	½ teaspoon salt
2 cups white bread flour	3 cups white bread flour	4 cups white bread flour
1½ teaspoons bread machine or active dry yeast	2¼ teaspoons bread machine or active dry yeast	2½ teaspoons bread machine or active dry yeast

1. Place the ingredients in your bread machine as recommended by the manufacturer.
2. Program the machine for Quick/Rapid bread and press Start.
3. When the loaf is done, remove the bucket from the machine.
4. Let the loaf cool for 5 minutes.
5. Gently shake the bucket to remove the loaf, and turn it out onto a rack to cool.

Cooking tip: Stir the shredded carrot into the other wet ingredients before adding the dry ingredients, so it is evenly distributed in the finished bread.

PER SERVING (1 SLICE): CALORIES: 161; TOTAL FAT: 4G; SATURATED FAT: 2G; CARBOHYDRATES: 28G; FIBER: 1G; SODIUM: 135MG; PROTEIN: 4G

Sauerkraut Rye Bread

PREP TIME IS 10 MINUTES OR LESS

Dense, strongly flavored, and dark describes this tasty loaf perfectly. Once the bread completely cools, you can cut thin slices similar to store-bought products. The sauerkraut provides stability to prevent the bread from crumbling and buckling.

8 SLICES / 1 POUND	12 SLICES / 1 ½ POUNDS	16 SLICES / 2 POUNDS
⅔ cups water, at 80°F to 90°F	1 cup water, at 80°F to 90°F	1¼ cups water, at 80°F to 90°F
1 tablespoon melted butter, cooled	1½ tablespoons melted butter, cooled	2 tablespoons melted butter, cooled
¼ cup molasses	⅓ cup molasses	½ cup molasses
¼ cup drained sauerkraut	½ cup drained sauerkraut	¾ cup drained sauerkraut
¼ teaspoon salt	⅓ teaspoon salt	½ teaspoon salt
1 tablespoon unsweetened cocoa powder	1½ tablespoons unsweetened cocoa powder	2 tablespoons unsweetened cocoa powder
Pinch ground nutmeg	Pinch ground nutmeg	Pinch ground nutmeg
½ cup rye flour	¾ cup rye flour	1 cup rye flour
1¼ cups white bread flour	2 cups white bread flour	2½ cups white bread flour
1⅛ teaspoons bread machine or instant yeast	1⅔ teaspoons bread machine or instant yeast	2¼ teaspoons bread machine or instant yeast

1. Place the ingredients in your bread machine as recommended by the manufacturer.

2. Program the machine for Basic/White bread, select light or medium crust, and press Start.

3. When the loaf is done, remove the bucket from the machine.

4. Let the loaf cool for 5 minutes.

5. Gently shake the bucket to remove the loaf, and turn it out onto a rack to cool.

Ingredient tip: Sauerkraut adds an interesting tang and moisture to this dark rye bread, creating the perfect foundation for a pastrami or smoked meat sandwich. Make sure you squeeze as much liquid as possible from the sauerkraut so the liquid-to-dry ingredients ratio is perfect.

PER SERVING (1 SLICE): CALORIES: 145; TOTAL FAT: 2G; SATURATED FAT: 1G; CARBOHYDRATES: 29G; FIBER: 3G; SODIUM: 120MG; PROTEIN: 4G

Savory Onion Bread

PREP TIME IS 10 MINUTES OR LESS

There is a double shot of onions in every bite of bread: delicate chives and stronger dried onion. The bread base is similar to a French bread, so try cutting thick slices to accompany a hearty meal of spaghetti or a thick beef stew.

8 SLICES / 1 POUND	12 SLICES / 1½ POUNDS	16 SLICES / 2 POUNDS
⅔ cups water, at 80°F to 90°F	1 cup water, at 80°F to 90°F	1¼ cups water, at 80°F to 90°F
2 tablespoons melted butter, cooled	3 tablespoons melted butter, cooled	¼ cup melted butter, cooled
1 tablespoon sugar	1½ tablespoons sugar	2 tablespoons sugar
¾ teaspoon salt	1⅛ teaspoons salt	1½ teaspoons salt
2 tablespoons dried minced onion	3 tablespoons dried minced onion	¼ cup dried minced onion
1 tablespoon chopped fresh chives	1½ tablespoons chopped fresh chives	2 tablespoons chopped fresh chives
2 cups plus 2 tablespoons white bread flour	3 cups plus 2 tablespoons white bread flour	4¼ cups white bread flour
1⅛ teaspoons bread machine or instant yeast	1⅔ teaspoons bread machine or instant yeast	2¼ teaspoons bread machine or instant yeast

1. Place the ingredients in your bread machine as recommended by the manufacturer.

2. Program the machine for Basic/White bread, select light or medium crust, and press Start.

3. When the loaf is done, remove the bucket from the machine.

4. Let the loaf cool for 5 minutes.

5. Gently shake the bucket to remove the loaf, and turn it out onto a rack to cool.

Ingredient tip: Dried onion comes in a small container found in the salad dressing aisle in most supermarkets, next to the bacon bits and croutons. If you can't find dried onion, cook thinly sliced onion in an oven preheated to 200°F until it is dry and easy to crumble.

PER SERVING (1 SLICE): CALORIES: 148; TOTAL FAT: 3G; SATURATED FAT: 2G; CARBOHYDRATES: 26G; FIBER: 1G; SODIUM: 216MG; PROTEIN: 4G

Tomato Herb Bread

PREP TIME IS 10 MINUTES OR LESS

The shocking color of this bread might startle you—it is very red with flecks of dark green. The base of the recipe is tomato sauce, so the taste will be distinctly tomato. Try using tomato herb bread for a decadent grilled cheese sandwich made in a skillet, panini press, or waffle maker.

8 SLICES / 1 POUND	12 SLICES / 1½ POUNDS	16 SLICES / 2 POUNDS
½ cup tomato sauce, at 80°F to 90°F	¾ cup tomato sauce, at 80°F to 90°F	1 cup tomato sauce, at 80°F to 90°F
½ tablespoon olive oil	¾ tablespoon olive oil	1 tablespoon olive oil
½ tablespoon sugar	¾ tablespoon sugar	1 tablespoon sugar
1 tablespoon dried basil	1½ tablespoons dried basil	2 tablespoons dried basil
½ tablespoon dried oregano	¾ tablespoon dried oregano	1 tablespoon dried oregano
½ teaspoon salt	¾ teaspoon salt	1 teaspoon salt
2 tablespoons grated Parmesan cheese	3 tablespoons grated Parmesan cheese	¼ cup grated Parmesan cheese
1½ cups white bread flour	2¼ cups white bread flour	3 cups white bread flour
1⅛ teaspoons bread machine or instant yeast	2 teaspoons bread machine or instant yeast	2¼ teaspoons bread machine or instant yeast

1. Place the ingredients in your bread machine as recommended by the manufacturer.
2. Program the machine for Basic/White bread, select light or medium crust, and press Start.
3. When the loaf is done, remove the bucket from the machine.
4. Let the loaf cool for 5 minutes.
5. Gently shake the bucket to remove the loaf, and turn it out onto a rack to cool.

Substitution tip: You can make your own tomato sauce by puréeing fresh tomatoes and then simmering them to remove some of the liquid. The taste and color will not be quite as intense as with a purchased sauce.

PER SERVING (1 SLICE): CALORIES: 110; TOTAL FAT: 2G; SATURATED FAT: 1G; CARBOHYDRATES: 20G; FIBER: 1G; SODIUM: 250MG; PROTEIN: 4G

Mashed Potato Bread

PREP TIME IS 20 MINUTES OR LESS

The last place you might consider using fluffy mashed potatoes is in bread, but this starchy vegetable creates an incredibly moist product that is fairly dense. The starch in the potatoes converts to sugar, which feeds the yeast and stops the bread from drying out while it sits.

8 SLICES / 1 POUND	12 SLICES / 1 ½ POUNDS	16 SLICES / 2 POUNDS
½ cup water, at 80°F to 90°F	¾ cup water, at 80°F to 90°F	1 cup water, at 80°F to 90°F
⅓ cup finely mashed potatoes, at room temperature	½ cup finely mashed potatoes, at room temperature	⅔ cup finely mashed potatoes, at room temperature
1 egg, at room temperature	1 egg, at room temperature	1 egg, at room temperature
2 tablespoons melted butter, cooled	¼ cup melted butter, cooled	½ cup melted butter, cooled
4 teaspoons honey	2 tablespoons honey	2⅔ tablespoons honey
⅔ teaspoon salt	1 teaspoon salt	1⅓ teaspoons salt
2 cups white bread flour	3 cups white bread flour	4 cups white bread flour
1⅓ teaspoons bread machine or instant yeast	2 teaspoons bread machine or instant yeast	2¼ teaspoons bread machine or instant yeast

1. Place the ingredients in your bread machine as recommended by the manufacturer.

2. Program the machine for Basic/White bread, select light or medium crust, and press Start.

3. When the loaf is done, remove the bucket from the machine.

4. Let the loaf cool for 5 minutes.

5. Gently shake the bucket to remove the loaf, and turn it out onto a rack to cool.

Cooking tip: Allow the potatoes to come to room temperature before adding them to the bread machine. This way, you won't hamper the yeast activity with too much heat or prevent the bread from rising with not enough heat if the potatoes are taken right out of the refrigerator.

PER SERVING (1 SLICE): CALORIES: 175; TOTAL FAT: 5G; SATURATED FAT: 3G; CARBOHYDRATES: 29G; FIBER: 1G; SODIUM: 251MG; PROTEIN: 4G

Confetti Bread

PREP TIME IS 10 MINUTES OR LESS

This festive bread has tiny flecks of color throughout the loaf. Use this bread for creamy egg or chicken salad sandwiches, then cut them into perfect quarters for a tea party or lunch. A variety of vegetables add nutrition and visual impact to this healthful, fiber-packed bread.

8 SLICES / 1 POUND

⅓ cup milk, at 80°F to 90°F

2 tablespoons water, at 80°F to 90°F

2 teaspoons melted butter, cooled

⅔ teaspoon white vinegar

4 teaspoons sugar

⅔ teaspoon salt

4 teaspoons grated Parmesan cheese

⅓ cup quick oats

1⅔ cups white bread flour

1 teaspoon bread machine or instant yeast

⅓ cup finely chopped zucchini

¼ cup finely chopped yellow bell pepper

¼ cup finely chopped red bell pepper

4 teaspoons chopped chives

12 SLICES / 1 ½ POUNDS

½ cup milk, at 80°F to 90°F

3 tablespoons water, at 80°F to 90°F

1 tablespoon melted butter, cooled

1 teaspoon white vinegar

2 tablespoons sugar

1 teaspoon salt

2 tablespoons grated Parmesan cheese

½ cup quick oats

2½ cups white bread flour

1½ teaspoons bread machine or instant yeast

½ cup finely chopped zucchini

¼ cup finely chopped yellow bell pepper

¼ cup finely chopped red bell pepper

2 tablespoons chopped chives

16 SLICES / 2 POUNDS

⅔ cup milk, at 80°F to 90°F

¼ cup water, at 80°F to 90°F

4 teaspoons melted butter, cooled

1⅓ teaspoons white vinegar

2⅔ tablespoons sugar

1⅓ teaspoons salt

2⅔ tablespoons grated Parmesan cheese

⅔ cup quick oats

3⅓ cups white bread flour

2 teaspoons bread machine or instant yeast

⅔ cup finely chopped zucchini

¼ cup finely chopped yellow bell pepper

¼ cup finely chopped red bell pepper

2⅔ tablespoons chopped chives

→

1. Place the ingredients, except the vegetables, in your bread machine as recommended by the manufacturer.
2. Program the machine for Basic/White bread, select light or medium crust, and press Start.
3. When the machine signals, add the chopped vegetables; if your machine has no signal, add the vegetables just before the second kneading is finished.
4. When the loaf is done, remove the bucket from the machine.
5. Let the loaf cool for 5 minutes.
6. Gently shake the bucket to remove the loaf, and turn it out onto a rack to cool.

Cooking tip: Make sure the chopped vegetables are patted dry with paper towels, so the extra moisture does not interfere with the bread rising.

PER SERVING (1 SLICE): CALORIES: 136; TOTAL FAT: 2G; SATURATED FAT: 1G; CARBOHYDRATES: 25G; FIBER: 1G; SODIUM: 218MG; PROTEIN: 4G

Pretty Borscht Bread

PREP TIME IS 10 MINUTES OR LESS

Your family will not realize that the pretty pink hue of the bread used for their sandwiches comes from healthy vegetables. Chicken salad, cream cheese, or aged Cheddar all taste fabulous combined with this bread. Try this bread at your next themed birthday party to delight your guests.

8 SLICES / 1 POUND	12 SLICES / 1½ POUNDS	16 SLICES / 2 POUNDS
½ cup water, at 80°F to 90°F	¾ cups water, at 80°F to 90°F	1 cup water, at 80°F to 90°F
½ cup grated raw beetroot	¾ cup grated raw beetroot	1 cup grated raw beetroot
1 tablespoon melted butter, cooled	1½ tablespoons melted butter, cooled	2 tablespoons melted butter, cooled
1 tablespoon sugar	1½ tablespoons sugar	2 tablespoons sugar
¾ teaspoon salt	1¼ teaspoons salt	2 teaspoons salt
2 cups white bread flour	3 cups white bread flour	4 cups white bread flour
¾ teaspoon bread machine or instant yeast	1¼ teaspoons bread machine or instant yeast	1⅔ teaspoons bread machine or instant yeast

1. Place the ingredients in your bread machine as recommended by the manufacturer.

2. Program the machine for Basic/White bread, select light or medium crust, and press Start.

3. When the loaf is done, remove the bucket from the machine.

4. Let the loaf cool for 5 minutes.

5. Gently shake the bucket to remove the loaf, and turn it out onto a rack to cool.

Variation tip: If the pinkish-red hue of this bread is not to your liking, you can use yellow beets instead. Use the exact same amount and same preparation as with the red variety.

PER SERVING (1 SLICE): CALORIES: 141; TOTAL FAT: 2G; SATURATED FAT: 1G; CARBOHYDRATES: 27G; FIBER: 1G; SODIUM: 268MG; PROTEIN: 4G

Yeasted Pumpkin Bread

PREP TIME IS 10 MINUTES OR LESS

Your family might assume you are making a pumpkin pie instead of bread when the scent of the baking loaf drifts throughout your home. If you can, wait until the bread is completely cooled before slicing it, so it doesn't fall apart. The flavor of pumpkin will also be stronger when the bread is no longer warm.

8 SLICES / 1 POUND

⅓ cup milk, at 80°F to 90°F

⅔ cup canned pumpkin

2 tablespoons melted butter, cooled

⅔ teaspoon grated ginger

2¾ tablespoons sugar

½ teaspoon salt

⅔ teaspoon ground cinnamon

¼ teaspoon ground cloves

2 cups white bread flour

1⅛ teaspoons bread machine or instant yeast

12 SLICES / 1½ POUNDS

½ cup milk, at 80°F to 90°F

1 cup canned pumpkin

3 tablespoons melted butter, cooled

1 teaspoon grated ginger

¼ cup plus 1 teaspoon sugar

¾ teaspoon salt

1 teaspoon ground cinnamon

¼ teaspoon ground cloves

3 cups white bread flour

1⅔ teaspoons bread machine or instant yeast

16 SLICES / 2 POUNDS

⅔ cup milk, at 80°F to 90°F

1⅓ cups canned pumpkin

¼ cup melted butter, cooled

1⅓ teaspoons grated ginger

5⅔ tablespoons sugar

1 teaspoon salt

1⅓ teaspoons ground cinnamon

⅓ teaspoon ground cloves

4 cups white bread flour

2¼ teaspoons bread machine or instant yeast

1. Place the ingredients in your bread machine as recommended by the manufacturer.
2. Program the machine for Basic/White bread, select light or medium crust, and press Start.
3. When the loaf is done, remove the bucket from the machine.
4. Let the loaf cool for 5 minutes.
5. Gently shake the bucket to remove the loaf, and turn it out onto a rack to cool.

Substitution tip: Ground ginger can be used instead of freshly grated ginger with marvelous results. Halve the amount of fresh ginger for each loaf, so you don't end up with too much gingery goodness.

PER SERVING (1 SLICE): CALORIES: 170; TOTAL FAT: 4G; SATURATED FAT: 2G; CARBOHYDRATES: 31G; FIBER: 2G; SODIUM: 175MG; PROTEIN: 4G

Oatmeal Zucchini Bread

PREP TIME IS 10 MINUTES OR LESS

This is not dainty bread with an airy texture. It is rustic and moist, with an almost undetectable zucchini flavor. If you want to make a dairy-free loaf, swap out the milk for the same amount of water. Thick slices of this bread would be an ideal choice to serve beside a bowl of thick stew or chili.

8 SLICES / 1 POUND	12 SLICES / 1½ POUNDS	16 SLICES / 2 POUNDS
⅓ cup milk, at 80°F to 90°F	½ cup milk, at 80°F to 90°F	⅔ cup milk, at 80°F to 90°F
½ cup finely shredded zucchini	¾ cup finely shredded zucchini	1 cup finely shredded zucchini
¼ teaspoon freshly squeezed lemon juice, at room temperature	¼ teaspoon freshly squeezed lemon juice, at room temperature	⅓ teaspoon freshly squeezed lemon juice, at room temperature
2 teaspoons olive oil	1 tablespoon olive oil	4 teaspoons olive oil
2 teaspoons sugar	1 tablespoon sugar	4 teaspoons sugar
⅔ teaspoon salt	1 teaspoon salt	1⅓ teaspoons salt
½ cup quick oats	¾ cup quick oats	1 cup quick oats
½ cup whole-wheat flour	¾ cup whole-wheat flour	1 cup whole-wheat flour
1 cup white bread flour	1½ cups white bread flour	2 cups white bread flour
1½ teaspoons bread machine or instant yeast	2¼ teaspoons bread machine or instant yeast	2¼ teaspoons bread machine or instant yeast

1. Place the ingredients in your bread machine as recommended by the manufacturer.
2. Program the machine for Basic/White bread, select light or medium crust, and press Start.
3. When the loaf is done, remove the bucket from the machine.
4. Let the loaf cool for 5 minutes.
5. Gently shake the bucket to remove the loaf, and turn it out onto a rack to cool.

Substitution tip: If you have yellow zucchini on hand instead of the more common green, it would be a fine addition to this loaf. Your bread will have yellow bits instead of green flecks when it is cut.

PER SERVING (1 SLICE): CALORIES: 127; TOTAL FAT: 2G; SATURATED FAT: 0G; CARBOHYDRATES: 23G; FIBER: 1G; SODIUM: 200MG; PROTEIN: 4G

Hot Red Pepper Bread

PREP TIME IS 10 MINUTES OR LESS

Grilled chicken breasts, steak sliced on the bias, and leftover turkey breast all pair beautifully with the heat and sweetness of this loaf. The finished taste will depend on the type of hot red pepper relish used in the recipe, so try a few to determine your favorite. You can even make your own relish to use for the bread and other recipes.

8 SLICES / 1 POUND	12 SLICES / 1½ POUNDS	16 SLICES / 2 POUNDS
¾ cup plus 1 tablespoon milk, at 80°F to 90°F	1¼ cups milk, at 80°F to 90°F	1⅔ cups milk, at 80°F to 90°F
2⅔ tablespoons red pepper relish	¼ cup red pepper relish	⅓ cup red pepper relish
4 teaspoons chopped roasted red pepper	2 tablespoons chopped roasted red pepper	2⅔ tablespoons chopped roasted red pepper
2 tablespoons melted butter, cooled	3 tablespoons melted butter, cooled	¼ cup melted butter, cooled
2 tablespoons light brown sugar	3 tablespoons light brown sugar	⅓ cup light brown sugar
⅔ teaspoon salt	1 teaspoon salt	1⅓ teaspoons salt
2 cups white bread flour	3 cups white bread flour	4 cups white bread flour
1 teaspoon bread machine or instant yeast	1½ teaspoons bread machine or instant yeast	2 teaspoons bread machine or instant yeast

1. Place the ingredients in your bread machine as recommended by the manufacturer.

2. Program the machine for Basic/White bread, select light or medium crust, and press Start.

3. When the loaf is done, remove the bucket from the machine.

4. Let the loaf cool for 5 minutes.

5. Gently shake the bucket to remove the loaf, and turn it out onto a rack to cool.

Ingredient tip: There is a very good chance you will have some red pepper relish left over after the loaf is baked. Besides using the condiment in another loaf, you could also use it in sauces, as a spread on sandwiches, as a topping for grilled steak, or even eat it by the spoon right out of the jar.

PER SERVING (1 SLICE): CALORIES: 167; TOTAL FAT: 4G; SATURATED FAT: 2G; CARBOHYDRATES: 28G; FIBER: 1G; SODIUM: 237MG; PROTEIN: 4G

French Onion Bread

PREP TIME IS 10 MINUTES OR LESS

Served warm out of the oven, this bread is an irresistible side dish that all your dinner guests will be reaching for until it's gone. In this recipe, the dough is mixed with onion flakes and fresh chives for maximum flavor. The chives add pretty green flecks to the appearance of the loaf and enhance it with a hint of garlic.

8 SLICES / 1 POUND	12 SLICES / 1½ POUNDS	16 SLICES / 2 POUNDS
¾ cup plus 1 tablespoon milk, at 80°F to 90°F	1¼ cups milk, at 80°F to 90°F	1⅔ cups milk, at 80°F to 90°F
2⅔ tablespoons melted butter, cooled	¼ cup melted butter, cooled	⅓ cup melted butter, cooled
2 tablespoons light brown sugar	3 tablespoons light brown sugar	⅓ cup light brown sugar
⅔ teaspoon salt	1 teaspoon salt	1⅓ teaspoons salt
2 tablespoons dehydrated onion flakes	3 tablespoons dehydrated onion flakes	¼ cup dehydrated onion flakes
4 teaspoons chopped fresh chives	2 tablespoons chopped fresh chives	2⅔ tablespoons chopped fresh chives
⅔ teaspoon garlic powder	1 teaspoon garlic powder	1⅓ teaspoons garlic powder
2 cups white bread flour	3 cups white bread flour	4 cups white bread flour
⅔ teaspoon bread machine or instant yeast	1 teaspoon bread machine or instant yeast	1⅔ teaspoons bread machine or instant yeast

1. Place the ingredients in your bread machine as recommended by the manufacturer.
2. Program the machine for Basic/White bread, select light or medium crust, and press Start.
3. When the loaf is done, remove the bucket from the machine.
4. Let the loaf cool for 5 minutes.
5. Gently shake the bucket to remove the loaf, and turn it out onto a rack to cool.

Variation tip: Sautéed onions that are patted dry and cooled would make a nice addition to this bread instead of the dehydrated product. The finished loaf will have onion pieces in it instead of just an onion flavor.

PER SERVING (1 SLICE): CALORIES: 172; TOTAL FAT: 5G; SATURATED FAT: 3G; CARBOHYDRATES: 28G; FIBER: 1G; SODIUM: 235MG; PROTEIN: 4G

Golden Butternut Squash Raisin Bread

PREP TIME IS 10 MINUTES OR LESS

Butternut squash is a wonderful side dish for special occasions or autumn meals. A whole squash makes quite a bit of mashed squash, so you'll probably have leftovers. Bread is one of the best ways to use up these leftovers as long as you haven't added too many other ingredients to your side dish. A little butter, sweetener, and spice are fine, but mini-marshmallows, nuts, or too much salt would affect the finished bread.

16 SLICES / 2 POUNDS

2 cups cooked mashed butternut squash, at room temperature

1 cup (2 sticks) butter, at room temperature

3 eggs, at room temperature

1 teaspoon pure vanilla extract

2 cups sugar

½ cup light brown sugar

3 cups all-purpose flour

1 teaspoon baking soda

1 teaspoon ground cinnamon

½ teaspoon ground cloves

½ teaspoon ground nutmeg

½ teaspoon salt

½ teaspoon baking powder

½ cup golden raisins

1. Place the butternut squash, butter, eggs, vanilla, sugar, and brown sugar in your bread machine.

2. Program the machine for Quick/Rapid bread and press Start.

3. While the wet ingredients are mixing, stir together the flour, baking soda, cinnamon, cloves, nutmeg, salt, and baking powder in a small bowl.

4. After the first fast mixing is done and the machine signals, add the dry ingredients and raisins.

5. When the loaf is done, remove the bucket from the machine.

6. Let the loaf cool for 5 minutes.

7. Gently shake the bucket to remove the loaf, and turn it out onto a rack to cool.

Substitution tip: Mashed cooked pumpkin or sweet potato would taste very similar to the squash in this recipe. You won't need to adjust the spices or sugar if you use either option.

PER SERVING (1 SLICE): CALORIES: 335; TOTAL FAT: 13G; SATURATED FAT: 8G; CARBOHYDRATES: 53G; FIBER: 1G; SODIUM: 251MG; PROTEIN: 4G

Sweet Potato Bread

PREP TIME IS 10 MINUTES OR LESS

The best sweet potatoes for this recipe are baked. Boiled potatoes soak up water, which changes the texture of the mash. Bake your sweet potatoes, scoop out the soft flesh while they are still warm, and mash it well. Make sure you let the mash come to room temperature before using it in the bread, or you might hamper the ability of the yeast to work.

12 TO 16 SLICES / 1½ TO 2 POUNDS

1½ cups mashed cooked sweet potato, at room temperature

¾ cup buttermilk, at room temperature

½ cup sugar

¼ cup melted butter, cooled

1 egg, at room temperature

1½ cups all-purpose flour

1 teaspoon ground cinnamon

½ teaspoon baking powder

½ teaspoon baking soda

¼ teaspoon ground cloves

¼ teaspoon salt

1. Place the sweet potato, buttermilk, sugar, butter, and egg in your bread machine.

2. Program the machine for Quick/Rapid bread and press Start.

3. While the wet ingredients are mixing, stir together the flour, cinnamon, baking powder, baking soda, cloves, and salt in a small bowl.

4. After the first fast mixing is done and the machine signals, add the dry ingredients.

5. When the loaf is done, remove the bucket from the machine.

6. Let the loaf cool for 5 minutes.

7. Gently shake the bucket to remove the loaf, and turn it out onto a rack to cool.

Decoration tip: Sprinkle chopped pecans or walnuts on top of the quick bread batter after all the mixing cycles are complete. The nuts will bake into the loaf and look lovely studding the surface.

PER SERVING (1 SLICE): CALORIES: 152; TOTAL FAT: 5G; SATURATED FAT: 2G; CARBOHYDRATES: 25G; FIBER: 1G; SODIUM: 159MG; PROTEIN: 3G

Potato Thyme Bread

PREP TIME IS 10 MINUTES OR LESS

Potato bread usually does not taste like potato, although there are some recipes that result in bread with a vague potato flavor. The potato is starchy and lends a tender texture to the finished bread. Wait until the loaf is completely cooled before cutting it, so the slices keep their shape.

8 SLICES / 1 POUND	12 SLICES / 1½ POUNDS	16 SLICES / 2 POUNDS
¾ cup plus 1 tablespoon milk, at 80°F to 90°F	1¼ cups milk, at 80°F to 90°F	1⅔ cups milk, at 80°F to 90°F
4 teaspoons melted butter, cooled	2 tablespoons melted butter, cooled	2⅔ tablespoons melted butter, cooled
2 teaspoons honey	1 tablespoon honey	4 teaspoons honey
1 teaspoon salt	1½ teaspoons salt	2 teaspoons salt
⅔ teaspoon dried thyme	1 teaspoon dried thyme	1½ teaspoons dried thyme
⅓ cup instant potato flakes	½ cup instant potato flakes	⅔ cup instant potato flakes
2 cups white bread flour	3 cups white bread flour	4 cups white bread flour
1⅓ teaspoons bread machine or instant yeast	2 teaspoons bread machine or instant yeast	2½ teaspoons bread machine or instant yeast

1. Place the ingredients in your bread machine as recommended by the manufacturer.
2. Program the machine for Basic/White bread, select light or medium crust, and press Start.
3. When the loaf is done, remove the bucket from the machine.
4. Let the loaf cool for 5 minutes.
5. Gently shake the bucket to remove the loaf, and turn it out onto a rack to cool.

Substitution tip: Do not replace the potato flakes with regular mashed potatoes in this recipe, or the balance between wet and dry ingredients will be skewed, and your finished loaf might not be exactly what you envisioned.

~~~~~~

PER SERVING (1 SLICE): CALORIES: 158; TOTAL FAT: 3G; SATURATED FAT: 2G; CARBOHYDRATES: 29G; FIBER: 1G; SODIUM: 319MG; PROTEIN: 5G

Light Corn Bread

PREP TIME IS 10 MINUTES OR LESS

Cornmeal is made by grinding up sweet corn. It is available in several varieties, depending on what type of corn is used, such as white, blue, or yellow. Do not use a coarser-ground product called polenta for this recipe or you will not achieve the airy texture in the loaf. Look for a medium cornmeal for the best results.

8 SLICES / 1 POUND	12 SLICES / 1 ½ POUNDS	16 SLICES / 2 POUNDS
½ cup milk, at 80°F to 90°F	¾ cup milk, at 80°F to 90°F	1 cup plus 2 tablespoons milk, at 80°F to 90°F
1 egg, at room temperature	1 egg, at room temperature	1 egg, at room temperature
1 ½ tablespoons butter, melted and cooled	2 ¼ tablespoons butter, melted and cooled	3 tablespoons butter, melted and cooled
1 ½ tablespoons honey	2 ¼ tablespoons honey	3 tablespoons honey
½ teaspoon salt	¾ teaspoon salt	1 teaspoon salt
¼ cup cornmeal	⅓ cup cornmeal	½ cup cornmeal
1 ¾ cups white bread flour	2 ⅔ cups white bread flour	3 ½ cups white bread flour
1 ¼ teaspoons bread machine or instant yeast	1 ¾ teaspoons bread machine or instant yeast	2 ½ teaspoons bread machine or instant yeast

1. Place the ingredients in your bread machine as recommended by the manufacturer.
2. Program the machine for Basic/White bread, select light or medium crust, and press Start.
3. When the loaf is done, remove the bucket from the machine.
4. Let the loaf cool for 5 minutes.
5. Gently shake the bucket to remove the loaf, and turn it out onto a rack to cool.

Variation tip: Unlike many corn bread recipes, this version is a proper yeast-risen creation. You can add cheese, walnuts, cranberries, or scallions to the dough with excellent results.

PER SERVING (1 SLICE): CALORIES: 159; TOTAL FAT: 3G; SATURATED FAT: 2G; CARBOHYDRATES: 28G; FIBER: 1G; SODIUM: 178MG; PROTEIN: 4G

—Chapter Eight—

SOURDOUGH BREADS

Simple Sourdough Starter

PREP TIME IS 10 MINUTES PLUS FERMENTING TIME

Sourdough starters are often kept in professional kitchens because the bread made with this mixture has a spectacular distinctive flavor. The timing for fermentation will vary depending on the humidity and temperature in your kitchen, so start this process at least a week before you want to make the bread.

MAKES 2 CUPS (32 SERVINGS)

2½ teaspoons active dry yeast

2 cups water, at 100°F to 110°F

2 cups all-purpose flour

1. In a large nonmetallic bowl, stir together the yeast, water, and flour.
2. Cover the bowl loosely and place it in a warm place to ferment for 4 to 8 days, stirring several times per day.
3. When the starter is bubbly and has a pleasant sour smell, it is ready to use.
4. Store the starter covered in the refrigerator until you wish to use it.

Cooking tip: The starter should be white. If it has any other color tinge, such as pink or orange, throw it away.

PER SERVING (1 SLICE): CALORIES: 27; TOTAL FAT: 0G; SATURATED FAT: 0G; CARBOHYDRATES: 6G; FIBER: 0G; SODIUM: 0MG; PROTEIN: 1G

No-Yeast Sourdough Starter

PREP TIME IS 10 MINUTES PLUS FERMENTING TIME

If you have never made a sourdough starter, the elastic texture of the mixture will seem like great fun. When you stir the starter, it will cling to the spoon and stretch. Make sure you use a wooden spoon for stirring because some metals can interfere with the fermentation process.

MAKES 4 CUPS (64 SERVINGS)

2 cups all-purpose flour

2 cups chlorine-free bottled water, at room temperature

1. Stir together the flour and water in a large glass bowl with a wooden spoon.
2. Loosely cover the bowl with plastic wrap and place it in a warm area for 3 to 4 days, stirring at least twice a day, or until bubbly.
3. Store the starter in the refrigerator in a covered glass jar, and stir it before using.
4. Replenish your starter by adding back the same amount you removed, in equal parts flour and water.

Ingredient tip: A sourdough starter needs to be fed with water and flour in equal parts once a week if you keep it in the refrigerator and every second day if you leave it out at room temperature. If you don't use the starter up, throw it away.

PER SERVING (1 SLICE): CALORIES: 14; TOTAL FAT: 0G; SATURATED FAT: 0G; CARBOHYDRATES: 3G; FIBER: 0G; SODIUM: 0MG; PROTEIN: 0G

No-Yeast Whole-Wheat Sourdough Starter

PREP TIME IS 10 MINUTES PLUS FERMENTING TIME

If you want to make completely whole-wheat bread, you will need a whole-wheat starter for the recipe. The starter can be made from any type of flour, including rye, which can be substituted here using the same amounts. You can also double the recipe if you want more of this lovely starter on hand.

MAKES 2 CUPS (32 SERVINGS)

1 cup whole-wheat flour, divided

1 cup chlorine-free bottled water, at room temperature, divided

½ teaspoon honey

1. Stir together ½ cup of flour, ½ cup of water, and the honey in a large glass bowl with a wooden spoon.
2. Loosely cover the bowl with plastic wrap and place it in a warm area for 5 days, stirring at least twice a day.
3. After 5 days, stir in the remaining ½ cup of flour and ½ cup of water.
4. Cover the bowl loosely again with plastic wrap and place it in a warm area.
5. When the starter has bubbles and foam on top, it is ready to use.
6. Store the starter in the refrigerator in a covered glass jar, and stir it before using.
7. If you use half, replenish the starter with ½ cup flour and ½ cup water.

"Did You Know?" It was once thought that capturing wild yeast from the air populated sourdough starters, but there are actually lots of microorganisms in unsterilized flour. All you need is flour and water to create a lovely starter for your bread-making needs.

PER SERVING (1 SLICE): CALORIES: 15; TOTAL FAT: 0G; SATURATED FAT: 0G; CARBOHYDRATES: 3G; FIBER: 0G; SODIUM: 0MG; PROTEIN: 0G

Basic Sourdough Bread

PREP TIME IS 10 MINUTES OR LESS

Sourdough bread has an incredible tangy taste that goes well with any dish or preparation. Dip this bread in a steaming bowl of soup or stew, make a stacked sandwich, or toast it with peanut butter. You might find yourself stocking your refrigerator regularly with a starter so you can bake a loaf whenever the notion strikes.

8 SLICES / 1 POUND	12 SLICES / 1½ POUNDS	16 SLICES / 2 POUNDS
1⅓ cups Simple Sourdough Starter (page 138), fed, active, and at room temperature	2 cups Simple Sourdough Starter (page 138), fed, active, and at room temperature	2⅔ cups Simple Sourdough Starter (page 138), fed, active, and at room temperature
4 teaspoons water, at 80°F to 90°F	2 tablespoons water, at 80°F to 90°F	2⅔ tablespoons water, at 80°F to 90°F
4 teaspoons melted butter, cooled	2 tablespoons melted butter, cooled	2⅔ tablespoons melted butter, cooled
1⅓ teaspoons sugar	2 teaspoons sugar	2⅔ teaspoons sugar
1 teaspoon salt	1½ teaspoons salt	2 teaspoons salt
1⅔ cups white bread flour	2½ cups white bread flour	3⅓ cups white bread flour
1 teaspoon bread machine or instant yeast	1½ teaspoons bread machine or instant yeast	2 teaspoons bread machine or instant yeast

1. Place the ingredients in your bread machine as recommended by the manufacturer.

2. Program the machine for Basic/White bread, select light or medium crust, and press Start.

3. When the loaf is done, remove the bucket from the machine.

4. Let the loaf cool for 5 minutes.

5. Gently shake the bucket to remove the loaf, and turn it out onto a rack to cool.

Substitution tip: Honey combines well with the tangy flavor of sourdough, so feel free to use this sweetener in place of the sugar. Brown sugar would also be an excellent choice.

PER SERVING (1 SLICE): CALORIES: 154; TOTAL FAT: 2G; SATURATED FAT: 1G; CARBOHYDRATES: 29G; FIBER: 1G; SODIUM: 305MG; PROTEIN: 4G

Whole-Wheat Sourdough Bread

PREP TIME IS 10 MINUTES OR LESS

If you are a whole-wheat enthusiast, you will really enjoy this bread. The texture is a little denser than a traditional sourdough, but the taste will still be familiar. If you need to use a sourdough starter made from all-purpose flour, the results will be the same.

8 SLICES / 1 POUND

⅔ cups water, at 80°F to 90°F

⅔ cup No-Yeast Whole-Wheat Sourdough Starter (page 140), fed, active, and at room temperature

4 teaspoons melted butter, cooled

2 teaspoons sugar

1 teaspoon salt

2 cups whole-wheat flour

1¼ teaspoons bread machine or instant yeast

12 SLICES / 1 ½ POUNDS

¾ cup plus 2 tablespoons water, at 80°F to 90°F

¾ cup plus 2 tablespoons No-Yeast Whole-Wheat Sourdough Starter (page 140), fed, active, and at room temperature

2 tablespoons melted butter, cooled

1 tablespoon sugar

1½ teaspoons salt

3 cups whole-wheat flour

1¾ teaspoons bread machine or instant yeast

16 SLICES / 2 POUNDS

1¼ cups water, at 80°F to 90°F

1¼ cups No-Yeast Whole-Wheat Sourdough Starter (page 140), fed, active, and at room temperature

2⅔ tablespoons melted butter, cooled

4 teaspoons sugar

2 teaspoons salt

4 cups whole-wheat flour

2½ teaspoons bread machine or instant yeast

1. Place the ingredients in your bread machine as recommended by the manufacturer.
2. Program the machine for Whole-Wheat/Whole-Grain bread, select light or medium crust, and press Start.
3. When the loaf is done, remove the bucket from the machine.
4. Let the loaf cool for 5 minutes.
5. Gently shake the bucket to remove the loaf, and turn it out onto a rack to cool.

Cooking tip: This bread is 100 percent whole-wheat, so it usually would not rise as much as one made with white bread flour that has more protein. However, the sourdough starter ensures a nice rise as long as you make sure it is at room temperature.

PER SERVING (1 SLICE): CALORIES: 155; TOTAL FAT: 2G; SATURATED FAT: 1G; CARBOHYDRATES: 29G; FIBER: 1G; SODIUM: 305MG; PROTEIN: 4G

Multigrain Sourdough Bread

PREP TIME IS 10 MINUTES OR LESS

The taste of multigrain breads will vary because most multigrain mixtures feature different combinations of grains. The signature sourdough flavor will still be evident but not as strong as bread made with white flour exclusively. This bread would be nice with a few tablespoons of sesame seeds in with the flour.

8 SLICES / 1 POUND	12 SLICES / 1 ½ POUNDS	16 SLICES / 2 POUNDS
⅓ cup plus 1 tablespoon water, at 80°F to 90°F	⅔ cup water, at 80°F to 90°F	¾ cup plus 1 tablespoon water, at 80°F to 90°F
½ cup Simple Sourdough Starter (page 138), fed, active, and at room temperature	¾ cup Simple Sourdough Starter (page 138), fed, active, and at room temperature	1 cup Simple Sourdough Starter (page 138), fed, active, and at room temperature
4 teaspoons melted butter, cooled	2 tablespoons melted butter, cooled	2⅔ tablespoons melted butter, cooled
1⅔ tablespoons sugar	2½ tablespoons sugar	3⅓ tablespoons sugar
½ teaspoon salt	¾ teaspoon salt	1 teaspoon salt
½ cup multigrain cereal (Bob's Red Mill or equivalent)	¾ cup multigrain cereal (Bob's Red Mill or equivalent)	1 cup multigrain cereal (Bob's Red Mill or equivalent)
1¾ cups white bread flour	2⅔ cups white bread flour	3½ cups white bread flour
1 teaspoon bread machine or instant yeast	1½ teaspoons bread machine or instant yeast	2 teaspoons bread machine or instant yeast

1. Place the ingredients in your bread machine as recommended by the manufacturer.
2. Program the machine for Whole-Wheat/Whole-Grain bread, select light or medium crust, and press Start.
3. When the loaf is done, remove the bucket from the machine.
4. Let the loaf cool for 5 minutes.
5. Gently shake the bucket to remove the loaf, and turn it out onto a rack to cool.

Substitution tip: There are quite a few types of multigrain flour available that are a mix of whole or chopped grains and actual flour. If you want to try 12-grain bread flour, use an amount that is equivalent to the amounts of the multigrain cereal and flour in this recipe.

PER SERVING (1 SLICE): CALORIES: 172; TOTAL FAT: 2G; SATURATED FAT: 1G; CARBOHYDRATES: 32G; FIBER: 2G; SODIUM: 162MG; PROTEIN: 14G

Faux Sourdough Bread

PREP TIME IS 10 MINUTES OR LESS

Sometimes you want a sourdough loaf and do not have a properly fermented starter ready to use, especially if this type of bread is a family favorite. When this happens, make faux sourdough bread. This bread is more tender than a standard loaf of sourdough, so wait until it cools completely before cutting the loaf into slices.

8 SLICES / 1 POUND	12 SLICES / 1 ½ POUNDS	16 SLICES / 2 POUNDS
½ cup plus 1 tablespoon water, at 80°F to 90°F	¾ cup plus 1 tablespoon water, at 80°F to 90°F	1 cup plus 2 tablespoons water, at 80°F to 90°F
¼ cup sour cream, at room temperature	⅓ cup sour cream, at room temperature	½ cup sour cream, at room temperature
1½ tablespoons melted butter, cooled	2¼ tablespoons melted butter, cooled	3 tablespoons melted butter, cooled
1 tablespoon apple cider vinegar	1½ tablespoons apple cider vinegar	2 tablespoons apple cider vinegar
½ tablespoon sugar	¾ tablespoon sugar	1 tablespoon sugar
½ teaspoon salt	¾ teaspoon salt	1 teaspoon salt
2 cups white bread flour	3 cups white bread flour	4 cups white bread flour
¾ teaspoon bread machine or instant yeast	1 teaspoon bread machine or instant yeast	1½ teaspoons bread machine or instant yeast

1. Place the ingredients in your bread machine as recommended by the manufacturer.
2. Program the machine for French bread, select light or medium crust, and press Start.
3. When the loaf is done, remove the bucket from the machine.
4. Let the loaf cool for 5 minutes.
5. Gently shake the bucket to remove the loaf, and turn it out onto a rack to cool.

Substitution tip: Plain white vinegar would work fine in lieu of apple cider vinegar in this recipe, even though the apple cider vinegar contains sugar. Use the same amount of white vinegar and enjoy the delicious results in your loaf of bread.

PER SERVING (1 SLICE): CALORIES: 151; TOTAL FAT: 4G; SATURATED FAT: 2G; CARBOHYDRATES: 25G; FIBER: 1G; SODIUM: 167; PROTEIN: 4G

Sourdough Milk Bread

PREP TIME IS 10 MINUTES OR LESS

Milk breads are tender and have a fine texture that seems to melt on the tongue. The sourdough taste in this variation makes the loaf seem sturdier and perfect for simple sandwiches. Wait until this bread is completely cooled to cut it, so the slices are even and keep their shape.

8 SLICES / 1 POUND	12 SLICES / 1 ½ POUNDS	16 SLICES / 2 POUNDS
1 cup Simple Sourdough Starter (page 138) or No-Yeast Sourdough Starter (page 139), fed, active, and at room temperature	1 ½ cups Simple Sourdough Starter (page 138) or No-Yeast Sourdough Starter (page 139), fed, active, and at room temperature	2 cups Simple Sourdough Starter (page 138) or No-Yeast Sourdough Starter (page 139), fed, active, and at room temperature
¼ cup milk, at 80°F to 90°F	⅓ cup milk, at 80°F to 90°F	½ cup milk, at 80°F to 90°F
2 tablespoons olive oil	3 tablespoons olive oil	¼ cup olive oil
1 tablespoon honey	1 ½ tablespoons honey	2 tablespoons honey
⅔ teaspoon salt	1 teaspoon salt	1 ⅓ teaspoons salt
2 cups white bread flour	3 cups white bread flour	4 cups white bread flour
¾ teaspoon bread machine or instant yeast	1 teaspoon bread machine or instant yeast	1 ⅓ teaspoons bread machine or instant yeast

1. Place the ingredients in your bread machine as recommended by the manufacturer.

2. Program the machine for Basic/White bread, select light or medium crust, and press Start.

3. When the loaf is done, remove the bucket from the machine.

4. Let the loaf cool for 5 minutes.

5. Gently shake the bucket to remove the loaf, and turn it out onto a rack to cool.

"Did You Know"? Sourdough usually has a robust texture with a generous distribution of small holes in the bread—perfect for catching melting butter when you toast it. However, the addition of milk and honey in this recipe creates a more delicate loaf.

PER SERVING (1 SLICE): CALORIES: 185; TOTAL FAT: 4G; SATURATED FAT: 1G; CARBOHYDRATES: 32G; FIBER: 1G; SODIUM: 198MG; PROTEIN: 4G

Lemon Sourdough Bread

PREP TIME IS 10 MINUTES OR LESS

There is a generous amount of honey in this bread to add sweetness to the strong, tart citrus flavor. You might have a hard time deciding if you want to use it to make a sandwich or serve slices of the bread for dessert. The best option is to do both!

8 SLICES / 1 POUND

½ cup Simple Sourdough Starter (page 138) or No-Yeast Sourdough Starter (page 139), fed, active, and at room temperature

½ cup water, at 80°F to 90°F

1 small egg, at room temperature

2 tablespoons butter, melted and cooled

¼ cup honey

1 teaspoon salt

1⅓ teaspoons lemon zest

1 teaspoon lime zest

¼ cup wheat germ

2 cups white bread flour

1⅛ teaspoons bread machine or instant yeast

12 SLICES / 1½ POUNDS

¾ cup Simple Sourdough Starter (page 138) or No-Yeast Sourdough Starter (page 139), fed, active, and at room temperature

¾ cup water, at 80°F to 90°F

1 egg, at room temperature

3 tablespoons butter, melted and cooled

⅓ cup honey

1½ teaspoons salt

2 teaspoons lemon zest

1½ teaspoons lime zest

⅓ cup wheat germ

3 cups white bread flour

1¾ teaspoons bread machine or instant yeast

16 SLICES / 2 POUNDS

1 cup Simple Sourdough Starter (page 138) or No-Yeast Sourdough Starter (page 139), fed, active, and at room temperature

1 cup water, at 80°F to 90°F

1 egg, at room temperature

¼ cup butter, melted and cooled

½ cup minus 1 tablespoon honey

2 teaspoons salt

2⅔ teaspoons lemon zest

2 teaspoons lime zest

½ cup minus 1 tablespoon wheat germ

4 cups white bread flour

2¼ teaspoons bread machine or instant yeast

1. Place the ingredients in your bread machine as recommended by the manufacturer.

2. Program the machine for Basic/White bread, select light or medium crust, and press Start.

3. When the loaf is done, remove the bucket from the machine.

4. Let the loaf cool for 5 minutes.

5. Gently shake the bucket to remove the loaf, and turn it out onto a rack to cool.

"Did You Know?" Wheat germ is the small, nutrient-containing center of the wheat kernel. It is only about 2.5 percent of the weight of the kernel but is a bountiful source of nutrition. Health benefits of wheat germ include a boost to the immune system and prevention of cancer and heart disease. In addition to breads, wheat germ can be added to many recipes, including desserts and smoothies.

PER SERVING (1 SLICE): CALORIES: 206; TOTAL FAT: 4G; SATURATED FAT: 2G; CARBOHYDRATES: 37G; FIBER: 2G; SODIUM: 319MG; PROTEIN: 6G

San Francisco Sourdough Bread

PREP TIME IS 10 MINUTES OR LESS

San Francisco sourdough is often formed into large, round loaves featuring a slashed top, which creates deep grooves in the baked loaf. You will not get that signature appearance out of your bread machine, but the taste will still be delightful. If you want the slashed look, take the dough out after the kneading cycle and bake it in a regular oven after letting the bread rise.

8 SLICES / 1 POUND

¾ cup Simple Sourdough Starter (page 138) or No-Yeast Sourdough Starter (page 139), fed, active, and at room temperature

⅓ cup water, at 80°F to 90°F

1½ tablespoons olive oil

1 teaspoon salt

4 teaspoons sugar

1 tablespoon skim milk powder

¼ cup whole-wheat flour

1¾ cups white bread flour

1⅛ teaspoons bread machine or instant yeast

12 SLICES / 1½ POUNDS

1 cup plus 2 tablespoons Simple Sourdough Starter (page 138) or No-Yeast Sourdough Starter (page 139), fed, active, and at room temperature

½ cup plus 1 tablespoon water, at 80°F to 90°F

2¼ tablespoons olive oil

1½ teaspoons salt

2 tablespoons sugar

1½ tablespoons skim milk powder

⅓ cup whole-wheat flour

2⅔ cups white bread flour

1⅔ teaspoons bread machine or instant yeast

16 SLICES / 2 POUNDS

1½ cups Simple Sourdough Starter (page 138) or No-Yeast Sourdough Starter (page 139), fed, active, and at room temperature

¾ cup water, at 80°F to 90°F

3 tablespoons olive oil

2 teaspoons salt

2¾ tablespoons sugar

2 tablespoons skim milk powder

½ cup whole-wheat flour

3½ cups white bread flour

2¼ teaspoons bread machine or instant yeast

1. Place the ingredients in your bread machine as recommended by the manufacturer.

2. Program the machine for French bread, select light or medium crust, and press Start.

3. When the loaf is done, remove the bucket from the machine.

4. Let the loaf cool for 5 minutes.

5. Gently shake the bucket to remove the loaf, and turn it out onto a rack to cool.

"Did You Know?" If you want to make a truly authentic San Francisco sourdough bread, use a starter that is created with no yeast. This was the method used when migrant workers made this tangy loaf that was popular during the California Gold Rush.

PER SERVING (1 SLICE): CALORIES: 167; TOTAL FAT: 3G; SATURATED FAT: 0G; CARBOHYDRATES: 31G; FIBER: 1G; SODIUM: 297MG; PROTEIN: 4G

Sourdough Beer Bread

PREP TIME IS 10 MINUTES OR LESS

Dishes such as fiery chili, thick beef stew, and creamy seafood chowder require robust bread for dipping and scooping. Look no further than this incredible loaf for all your dipping needs. The beer and sourdough starter create a tangy flavor and high-rising loaf.

8 SLICES / 1 POUND

⅔ cup Simple Sourdough Starter (page 138) or No-Yeast Sourdough Starter (page 139), fed, active, and at room temperature

⅓ cup dark beer, at 80°F to 90°F

1 tablespoon melted butter, cooled

1½ teaspoons sugar

¾ teaspoon salt

1¾ cups white bread flour

¾ teaspoon bread machine or instant yeast

12 SLICES / 1½ POUNDS

1 cup Simple Sourdough Starter (page 138) or No-Yeast Sourdough Starter (page 139), fed, active, and at room temperature

½ cup plus 1 tablespoon dark beer, at 80°F to 90°F

1½ tablespoons melted butter, cooled

¾ tablespoon sugar

1⅛ teaspoons salt

2⅔ cups white bread flour

1⅛ teaspoons bread machine or instant yeast

16 SLICES / 2 POUNDS

1⅓ cups Simple Sourdough Starter (page 138) or No-Yeast Sourdough Starter (page 139), fed, active, and at room temperature

¾ cup dark beer, at 80°F to 90°F

2 tablespoons melted butter, cooled

1 tablespoon sugar

1½ teaspoons salt

3½ cups white bread flour

1½ teaspoons bread machine or instant yeast

1. Place the ingredients in your bread machine as recommended by the manufacturer.

2. Program the machine for French bread, select light or medium crust, and press Start.

3. When the loaf is done, remove the bucket from the machine.

4. Let the loaf cool for 5 minutes.

5. Gently shake the bucket to remove the loaf, and turn it out onto a rack to cool.

Cooking tip: Allow your beer to go flat if you are using a lager or lighter ale, so your bread does not rise too much. Darker beer is often flatter than regular brews, which is why it is used in this recipe.

PER SERVING (1 SLICE): CALORIES: 141; TOTAL FAT: 2G; SATURATED FAT: 1G; CARBOHYDRATES: 26G; FIBER: 1G; SODIUM: 205MG; PROTEIN: 4G

Crusty Sourdough Bread

PREP TIME IS 10 MINUTES OR LESS

The crust on this bread is absolutely addictive because it is thick, lightly flaky, and tangy from the sourdough starter. Do not be surprised if someone cuts off the top, sides, and bottom of the loaf, leaving the soft center. Try slices of this bread spread with homemade jam or red pepper relish.

8 SLICES / 1 POUND	12 SLICES / 1½ POUNDS	16 SLICES / 2 POUNDS
⅔ cup Simple Sourdough Starter (page 138), fed, active, and at room temperature	1 cup Simple Sourdough Starter (page 138), fed, active, and at room temperature	1⅓ cups Simple Sourdough Starter (page 138), fed, active, and at room temperature
⅓ cup water, at 80°F to 90°F	½ cup water, at 80°F to 90°F	⅔ cup water, at 80°F to 90°F
4 teaspoons honey	2 tablespoons honey	2⅔ tablespoons honey
1 teaspoon salt	1½ teaspoons salt	2 teaspoons salt
2 cups white bread flour	3 cups white bread flour	4 cups white bread flour
¾ teaspoon bread machine or instant yeast	1 teaspoon bread machine or instant yeast	1⅓ teaspoons bread machine or instant yeast

1. Place the ingredients in your bread machine as recommended by the manufacturer.

2. Program the machine for Basic/White bread, select light or medium crust, and press Start.

3. When the loaf is done, remove the bucket from the machine.

4. Let the loaf cool for 5 minutes.

5. Gently shake the bucket to remove the loaf, and turn it out onto a rack to cool.

Variation tip: The crust on this loaf is very similar to artisan breads—thick and robust. If you want an authentic artisan bread presentation, remove the dough after the kneading cycle, let it rise on a baking sheet, and bake it in a regular oven.

PER SERVING (1 SLICE): CALORIES: 144; TOTAL FAT: 0G; SATURATED FAT: 0G; CARBOHYDRATES: 31G; FIBER: 1G; SODIUM: 292MG; PROTEIN: 4G

Sourdough Cheddar Bread

PREP TIME IS 10 MINUTES OR LESS

Oat bran and whole-wheat flour pair nicely with the tangy sourdough starter and sharp Cheddar in this bread. The texture of the loaf may be different than any sourdough you have had before because of the added fiber. The cheese melts right into the dough, so you will get the flavor of Cheddar in every bite.

8 SLICES / 1 POUND

1 tablespoon melted butter, cooled

⅔ cup Simple Sourdough Starter (page 138) or No-Yeast Sourdough Starter (page 139), fed, active, and at room temperature

¼ cup water, at 80°F to 90°F

2⅔ teaspoons sugar

⅔ teaspoon salt

⅓ cup grated aged Cheddar cheese

⅔ cup whole-wheat flour

2⅔ tablespoons oat bran

¾ cup plus 1 tablespoon white bread flour

1 teaspoon bread machine or instant yeast

12 SLICES / 1½ POUNDS

1 cup Simple Sourdough Starter (page 138) or No-Yeast Sourdough Starter (page 139), fed, active, and at room temperature

⅓ cup water, at 80°F to 90°F

4 teaspoons sugar

1 teaspoon salt

½ cup (2 ounces) grated aged Cheddar cheese

⅔ cup whole-wheat flour

¼ cup oat bran

1⅓ cups white bread flour

1½ teaspoons bread machine or instant yeast

16 SLICES / 2 POUNDS

1⅓ cups Simple Sourdough Starter (page 138) or No-Yeast Sourdough Starter (page 139), fed, active, and at room temperature

½ cup minus 1 tablespoon water, at 80°F to 90°F

5⅓ teaspoons sugar

1⅓ teaspoons salt

⅔ cup (2½ ounces) grated aged Cheddar cheese

¾ cup plus 1 tablespoon whole-wheat flour

⅓ cup oat bran

1¾ cups white bread flour

2 teaspoons bread machine or instant yeast

1. Place the ingredients in your bread machine as recommended by the manufacturer.
2. Program the machine for Basic/White bread, select light or medium crust, and press Start.
3. When the loaf is done, remove the bucket from the machine.
4. Let the loaf cool for 5 minutes.
5. Gently shake the bucket to remove the loaf, and turn it out onto a rack to cool.

Substitution tip: Any type of cheese would be delicious in this recipe when combined with the tangy flavor of sourdough. More assertive-flavored cheeses may be the best choice because whole-wheat flour and oat bran have a stronger flavor than white flour.

PER SERVING (1 SLICE): CALORIES: 113; TOTAL FAT: 2G; SATURATED FAT: 1G; CARBOHYDRATES: 20G; FIBER: 1G; SODIUM: 234MG; PROTEIN: 4G

Herb Sourdough

PREP TIME IS 10 MINUTES OR LESS

Even the staff of life can be enhanced with fresh herbs. Nothing tastes more delicious than freshly baked bread made with herbs, perhaps even from your garden. The combinations and variations are infinite. This aromatic bread would be especially delicious served with dinner.

8 SLICES / 1 POUND	12 SLICES / 1½ POUNDS	16 SLICES / 2 POUNDS
1⅓ cups No-Yeast Sourdough Starter (page 139), fed, active, and at room temperature	2 cups No-Yeast Sourdough Starter (page 139), fed, active, and at room temperature	2⅔ cups No-Yeast Sourdough Starter (page 139), fed, active, and at room temperature
4 teaspoons water, at 80°F to 90°F	2 tablespoons water, at 80°F to 90°F	2⅔ tablespoons water, at 80°F to 90°F
4 teaspoons melted butter, cooled	2 tablespoons melted butter, cooled	2⅔ tablespoons melted butter, cooled
1⅓ teaspoons sugar	2 teaspoons sugar	2⅔ teaspoons sugar
1 teaspoon salt	1½ teaspoons salt	2 teaspoons salt
1 teaspoon chopped fresh basil	1½ teaspoons chopped fresh basil	2 teaspoons chopped fresh basil
1 teaspoon chopped fresh oregano	1½ teaspoons chopped fresh oregano	2 teaspoons chopped fresh oregano
½ teaspoon chopped fresh thyme	1 teaspoon chopped fresh thyme	1 teaspoon chopped fresh thyme
1⅔ cups white bread flour	2½ cups white bread flour	3⅓ cups white bread flour
1 teaspoon bread machine or instant yeast	1½ teaspoons bread machine or instant yeast	2 teaspoons bread machine or instant yeast

1. Place the ingredients in your bread machine as recommended by the manufacturer.
2. Program the machine for Basic/White bread, select light or medium crust, and press Start.
3. When the loaf is done, remove the bucket from the machine.
4. Let the loaf cool for 5 minutes.
5. Gently shake the bucket to remove the loaf, and turn it out onto a rack to cool.

Variation tip: As with most other herb breads, the combinations listed in the ingredients are just a suggestion. Use the same amounts of your favorite herbs and enjoy the wonderful smell while the bread bakes.

PER SERVING (1 SLICE): CALORIES: 155; TOTAL FAT: 2G; SATURATED FAT: 1G; CARBOHYDRATES: 29G; FIBER: 1G; SODIUM: 305MG; PROTEIN: 4G

Cranberry Pecan Sourdough

PREP TIME IS 10 MINUTES OR LESS

This is pretty bread dotted with red berries and lightly spiced with cinnamon. Chicken, turkey, cheese, and nut butters would be an excellent pairing with slices of this gently tangy bread. It would also make excellent toast for breakfast, sliced very thin and spread with butter or cream cheese.

8 SLICES / 1 POUND	12 SLICES / 1½ POUNDS	16 SLICES / 2 POUNDS
1⅓ cups No-Yeast Sourdough Starter (page 139), fed, active, and at room temperature	2 cups No-Yeast Sourdough Starter (page 139), fed, active, and at room temperature	2⅔ cups No-Yeast Sourdough Starter (page 139), fed, active, and at room temperature
4 teaspoons water, at 80°F to 90°F	2 tablespoons water, at 80°F to 90°F	2⅔ tablespoons water, at 80°F to 90°F
4 teaspoons melted butter, cooled	2 tablespoons melted butter, cooled	2⅔ tablespoons melted butter, cooled
1⅓ teaspoons sugar	2 teaspoons sugar	2⅔ teaspoons sugar
1 teaspoon salt	1½ teaspoons salt	2 teaspoons salt
¼ teaspoon ground cinnamon	⅓ teaspoon ground cinnamon	½ teaspoon ground cinnamon
1⅔ cups white bread flour	2½ cups white bread flour	3⅓ cups white bread flour
1 teaspoon bread machine or instant yeast	1½ teaspoons bread machine or instant yeast	2 teaspoons bread machine or instant yeast
¼ cup dried cranberries	⅓ cup dried cranberries	½ cup dried cranberries
¼ cup chopped pecans	⅓ cup chopped pecans	½ cup chopped pecans

1. Place the ingredients, except the cranberries and pecans, in your bread machine as recommended by the manufacturer.

2. Program the machine for Basic/White bread, select light or medium crust, and press Start.

3. Add the cranberries and pecans when the machine signals or 5 minutes before the second kneading cycle is finished.

4. When the loaf is done, remove the bucket from the machine.

5. Let the loaf cool for 5 minutes.

6. Gently shake the bucket to remove the loaf, and turn it out onto a rack to cool.

"Did You Know?" Cranberries are native to North America and one of the only fruits that holds this distinction. Cranberries take more than 16 months to ripen, and vines often hold many berries in different stages of maturation at the same time.

PER SERVING (1 SLICE): CALORIES: 156; TOTAL FAT: 2G; SATURATED FAT: 1G; CARBOHYDRATES: 29G; FIBER: 1G; SODIUM: 305MG; PROTEIN: 4G

Dark Chocolate Sourdough

PREP TIME IS 10 MINUTES OR LESS

This is not overly sweet bread despite the chocolate and raisins because there is a generous amount of cocoa powder in the recipe. The closest cousin to this loaf is Russian black bread in appearance and dark chocolate biscotti in taste. If you want to highlight the bitter cocoa taste, exclude the chocolate chips.

8 SLICES / 1 POUND	12 SLICES / 1½ POUNDS	16 SLICES / 2 POUNDS
1⅓ cups No-Yeast Sourdough Starter (page 139), fed, active, and at room temperature	2 cups No-Yeast Sourdough Starter (page 139), fed, active, and at room temperature	2⅔ cups No-Yeast Sourdough Starter (page 139), fed, active, and at room temperature
4 teaspoons water, at 80°F to 90°F	2 tablespoons water, at 80°F to 90°F	2⅔ tablespoons water, at 80°F to 90°F
4 teaspoons melted butter, cooled	2 tablespoons melted butter, cooled	2⅔ tablespoons melted butter, cooled
½ teaspoon pure vanilla extract	¾ teaspoon pure vanilla extract	1 teaspoon pure vanilla extract
1⅓ teaspoons sugar	2 teaspoons sugar	2⅔ teaspoons sugar
1 teaspoon salt	1½ teaspoons salt	2 teaspoons salt
¼ teaspoon ground cinnamon	⅓ teaspoon ground cinnamon	½ teaspoon ground cinnamon
2 tablespoons unsweetened cocoa powder	¼ cup unsweetened cocoa powder	¼ cup unsweetened cocoa powder
1⅔ cups white bread flour	2½ cups white bread flour	3⅓ cups white bread flour
1 teaspoon bread machine or instant yeast	1½ teaspoons bread machine or instant yeast	2 teaspoons bread machine or instant yeast
¼ cup semisweet chocolate chips	½ cup semisweet chocolate chips	¾ cup semisweet chocolate chips
¼ cup chopped pistachios	⅓ cup chopped pistachios	½ cup chopped pistachios
¼ cup raisins	⅓ cup raisins	½ cup raisins

1. Place the ingredients, except the chocolate chips, pistachios, and raisins, in your bread machine as recommended by the manufacturer.

2. Program the machine for Basic/White bread, select light or medium crust, and press Start.

3. Add the chocolate chips, pistachios, and raisins when the machine signals or 5 minutes before the second kneading cycle is finished.

4. When the loaf is done, remove the bucket from the machine.

5. Let the loaf cool for 5 minutes.

6. Gently shake the bucket to remove the loaf, and turn it out onto a rack to cool.

Variation tip: This is a great loaf to bake in a regular oven if you have the time. It is perfectly fine popping out of the bucket of your bread machine, but the dense texture of the finished bread seems to lend itself to a free-formed, rustic loaf.

PER SERVING (1 SLICE): CALORIES: 222; TOTAL FAT: 6G; SATURATED FAT: 2G; CARBOHYDRATES: 39G; FIBER: 2G; SODIUM: 356MG; PROTEIN: 5G

—*Chapter Nine*—

CREATIVE COMBINATION BREADS

Zucchini Pecan Bread

PREP TIME IS 10 MINUTES OR LESS

Even people who have no green thumb often have a proliferation of zucchini if they grow it in the garden. This means lots of different dishes to use up the vegetable, including moist breads. If you purchase your zucchini instead of growing it, scrub the skin well to remove any pesticide residue.

12 TO 16 SLICES / 1 ½ TO 2 POUNDS

2 eggs, at room temperature

½ cup melted butter, cooled

¾ cup shredded zucchini

½ cup packed light brown sugar

2 tablespoons sugar

1½ cups all-purpose flour

1 teaspoon ground cinnamon

½ teaspoon salt

½ teaspoon baking powder

½ teaspoon baking soda

¼ teaspoon ground allspice

½ cup chopped pecans

1. Place the ingredients in your bread machine as recommended by the manufacturer.
2. Program the machine for Quick/Rapid bread and press Start.
3. When the mixing is done, use a rubber spatula to scrape down the sides of the bucket, then stir.
4. When the loaf is done, remove the bucket from the machine.
5. Let the loaf cool for 5 minutes.
6. Gently shake the bucket to remove the loaf, and turn it out onto a rack to cool.
7. Wrap the loaf in plastic wrap after it is completely cooled and store it in the refrigerator.

Variation tip: Dates, walnuts, raisins, dried apple, and chopped hazelnuts can all be added to this sweet, lightly spiced bread. Make sure you don't add more than about 1 cup in total, or you might not be able to cut the finished bread without it falling apart.

PER SERVING (1 SLICE): CALORIES: 171; TOTAL FAT: 9G; SATURATED FAT: 5G; CARBOHYDRATES: 21G; FIBER: 1G; SODIUM: 218MG; PROTEIN: 3G

Raisin Bran Bread

PREP TIME IS 10 MINUTES OR LESS

Raisins and bran are a perfect pairing for a sweet and satisfying loaf of bread, topped with cinnamon butter or a little marmalade. Thin slices of Swiss cheese would also pair well with the raisins in a sandwich for lunch. This bread freezes beautifully if you want to make a couple of loaves.

8 SLICES / 1 POUND	12 SLICES / 1 ½ POUNDS	16 SLICES / 2 POUNDS
¾ cup milk, at 80°F to 90°F	1 ⅛ cup milk, at 80°F to 90°F	1 ½ cups milk, at 80°F to 90°F
1 ½ tablespoons melted butter, cooled	2 ¼ tablespoons melted butter, cooled	3 tablespoons melted butter, cooled
2 tablespoons sugar	3 tablespoons sugar	¼ cup sugar
1 teaspoon salt	1 ½ teaspoons salt	2 teaspoons salt
¼ cup wheat bran	⅓ cup wheat bran	½ cup wheat bran
1 ¾ cups white bread flour	2 ⅔ cups white bread flour	3 ½ cups white bread flour
1 teaspoon bread machine or instant yeast	1 ½ teaspoons bread machine or instant yeast	2 teaspoons bread machine or instant yeast
½ cup raisins	¾ cup raisins	1 cup raisins

1. Place the ingredients, except the raisins, in your bread machine as recommended by the manufacturer.
2. Program the machine for Basic/White bread, select light or medium crust, and press Start.
3. When the machine signals, add the raisins, or put them in the nut/raisin hopper and let your machine add them automatically.
4. When the loaf is done, remove the bucket from the machine.
5. Let the loaf cool for 5 minutes.
6. Gently shake the bucket to remove the loaf, and turn it out onto a rack to cool.

"Did You Know?" Bran is not a grain but the outer husk of many types of cereal grains. This incredible source of fiber was actually considered to be waste in mills before the 1970s when its health benefits were discovered.

PER SERVING (1 SLICE): CALORIES: 173; TOTAL FAT: 3G; SATURATED FAT: 2G; CARBOHYDRATES: 34G; FIBER: 2G; SODIUM: 317MG; PROTEIN: 4G

Lemon Poppy Seed Bread

PREP TIME IS 10 MINUTES OR LESS

The combination of lemon and poppy seed is common and often found in muffins, cakes, and breads. The freshness of lemon combines beautifully with the nutty, pleasant taste of poppy seeds. The speckling from the seeds looks pretty alongside the flecks of yellow lemon rind.

8 SLICES / 1 POUND

½ cup water, at 80°F to 90°F

1 egg, at room temperature, cooled

3 tablespoons freshly squeezed lemon juice, at room temperature

2 tablespoons melted butter, cooled

2 tablespoons sugar

2 teaspoons lemon zest

¾ teaspoon salt

2 cups white bread flour

1½ tablespoons poppy seeds

1 teaspoon bread machine or instant yeast

12 SLICES / 1 ½ POUNDS

¾ cup water, at 80°F to 90°F

1 egg, at room temperature

¼ cup freshly squeezed lemon juice, at room temperature

3 tablespoons melted butter, cooled

3 tablespoons sugar

2 teaspoons lemon zest

1 teaspoon salt

3 cups white bread flour

2 tablespoons poppy seeds

1¼ teaspoons bread machine or instant yeast

16 SLICES / 2 POUNDS

1 cup water, at 80°F to 90°F

1 egg, at room temperature

⅓ cup freshly squeezed lemon juice, at room temperature

¼ cup melted butter, cooled

¼ cup sugar

1 tablespoon lemon zest

1⅓ teaspoons salt

4 cups white bread flour

3 tablespoons poppy seeds

1¾ teaspoons bread machine or instant yeast

1. Place the ingredients in your bread machine as recommended by the manufacturer.
2. Program the machine for Basic/White bread, select light or medium crust, and press Start.
3. When the loaf is done, remove the bucket from the machine.
4. Let the loaf cool for 5 minutes.
5. Gently shake the bucket to remove the loaf, and turn it out onto a rack to cool.

"Did You Know?" Poppy seed is an oilseed obtained from the opium poppy. The seeds are very safe to use in food and contain negligible quantities of toxic alkaloids found in the opium poppy. They are widely used in baked goods such as rolls, bagels, sweet breads, biscuits, and cakes, and they are even used in dips and curries in India and Pakistan.

PER SERVING (1 SLICE): CALORIES: 167; TOTAL FAT: 4G; SATURATED FAT: 2G; CARBOHYDRATES: 28G; FIBER: 1G; SODIUM: 223MG; PROTEIN: 4G

Mustard Rye Bread

PREP TIME IS 10 MINUTES OR LESS

Adding the mustard directly into the rye bread in this recipe is an inspired strategy considering how delicious this combination is in sandwiches. Dijon mustard is a blend of brown mustard seeds, white wine, and spices. This condiment is produced in the Dijon region of France, and authentic products have a capital "D" in Dijon on the label.

8 SLICES / 1 POUND	12 SLICES / 1 ½ POUNDS	16 SLICES / 2 POUNDS
¾ cup plus 1 tablespoon water, at 80°F to 90°F	1 ¼ cups water, at 80°F to 90°F	1 ⅔ cups water, at 80°F to 90°F
2 ⅔ tablespoons Dijon mustard	¼ cup Dijon mustard	¼ cup plus 4 teaspoons Dijon mustard
1 tablespoon melted butter, cooled	1 ½ tablespoons melted butter, cooled	2 tablespoons melted butter, cooled
2 teaspoons sugar	1 tablespoon sugar	4 teaspoons sugar
½ teaspoon salt	¾ teaspoon salt	1 teaspoon salt
1 cup rye flour	1 ½ cups rye flour	2 cups rye flour
1 ⅓ cups white bread flour	2 cups white bread flour	2 ⅔ cups white bread flour
¾ teaspoon bread machine or instant yeast	1 teaspoon bread machine or instant yeast	1 ½ teaspoons bread machine or instant yeast

1. Place the ingredients in your bread machine as recommended by the manufacturer.

2. Program the machine for Basic/White bread, select light or medium crust, and press Start.

3. When the loaf is done, remove the bucket from the machine.

4. Let the loaf cool for 5 minutes.

5. Gently shake the bucket to remove the loaf, and turn it out onto a rack to cool.

Variation tip: Honey mustard or prepared hot mustard could replace the Dijon in the recipe. Honey mustard can be used in the same amount as the Dijon, but if you are using Keen's, you might want to reduce the Dijon amount by half.

PER SERVING (1 SLICE): CALORIES: 149; TOTAL FAT: 2G; SATURATED FAT: 1G; CARBOHYDRATES: 28G; FIBER: 4G; SODIUM: 217MG; PROTEIN: 5G

Ham and Cheese Bread

PREP TIME IS 10 MINUTES OR LESS

Make a loaf of this bread for a fresh twist on the traditional ham and cheese sandwich. Black Forest ham is a great choice to use in this recipe because it does not add too much additional salt. You can also use leftover roasted ham after the holidays.

8 SLICES / 1 POUND	12 SLICES / 1½ POUNDS	16 SLICES / 2 POUNDS
⅔ cup water, at 80°F to 90°F	1 cup plus 2 tablespoons water, at 80°F to 90°F	1½ cups water, at 80°F to 90°F
4 teaspoons sugar	2 tablespoons sugar	2¾ tablespoons sugar
1 teaspoon salt	1½ teaspoons salt	2 teaspoons salt
1½ teaspoons dried oregano	2 teaspoons dried oregano	2¾ teaspoons dried oregano
⅓ cup shredded Swiss cheese	½ cup (2 ounces) shredded Swiss cheese	⅔ cup (2½ ounces) shredded Swiss cheese
2¼ cups white bread flour	3¼ cups white bread flour	4¼ cups white bread flour
1 teaspoon bread machine or active dry yeast	1½ teaspoons bread machine or active dry yeast	2 teaspoons bread machine or active dry yeast
½ cup diced smoked ham	⅔ cup diced smoked ham	1 cup diced smoked ham

1. Place the ingredients, except the ham, in your bread machine as recommended by the manufacturer.
2. Program the machine for Basic/White bread, select light or medium crust, and press Start.
3. Add the ham about 5 minutes before the second kneading cycle ends.
4. When the loaf is done, remove the bucket from the machine.
5. Let the loaf cool for 5 minutes.
6. Gently shake the bucket to remove the loaf, and turn it out onto a rack to cool.

Cooking tip: Pat the ham slices completely dry with paper towels before dicing them, or you might end up with soggy sections in your finished bread.

PER SERVING (1 SLICE): CALORIES: 163; TOTAL FAT: 2G; SATURATED FAT: 1G; CARBOHYDRATES: 29G; FIBER: 1G; SODIUM: 397MG; PROTEIN: 6G

Sausage Herb Bread

PREP TIME IS 10 MINUTES OR LESS

At the end of the day, what is better than warm, fresh bread with pockets of sausage and a smattering of herbs? Not much. Roasted red pepper, goat cheese, and shredded spinach would make a marvelous filling between two slices of this bread.

8 SLICES / 1 POUND	12 SLICES / 1½ POUNDS	16 SLICES / 2 POUNDS
⅔ cup water, 80°F to 90°F	1 cup water, at 80°F to 90°F	1¼ cups plus 2 tablespoons water, at 80°F to 90°F
1 tablespoon olive oil	1½ tablespoons olive oil	2 tablespoons olive oil
1 tablespoon sugar	1½ tablespoons sugar	2 tablespoons sugar
¾ teaspoon salt	1⅛ teaspoons salt	1½ teaspoons salt
¼ teaspoon dried basil	⅓ teaspoon dried basil	½ teaspoon dried basil
¼ teaspoon dried oregano	⅓ teaspoon dried oregano	½ teaspoon dried oregano
⅓ cup cooked chopped Italian sausage	½ cup cooked chopped Italian sausage	¾ cup cooked chopped Italian sausage
2 cups white bread flour	3 cups white bread flour	4 cups white bread flour
1 teaspoon bread machine or instant yeast	1½ teaspoons bread machine or instant yeast	2 teaspoons bread machine or instant yeast

1. Place the ingredients in your bread machine as recommended by the manufacturer.
2. Program the machine for Basic/White bread, select light or medium crust, and press Start.
3. When the loaf is done, remove the bucket from the machine.
4. Let the loaf cool for 5 minutes.
5. Gently shake the bucket to remove the loaf, and turn it out onto a rack to cool.

Substitution tip: Italian sausage comes in many different varieties. German sausage, hot Italian sausage, fennel sausage, or honey-garlic sausage could all be chopped up and combined with the herbs in this bread. Drain the sausage well and pat away any extra grease with paper towels before you place it in the bread machine.

PER SERVING (1 SLICE): CALORIES: 143; TOTAL FAT: 3G; SATURATED FAT: 1G; CARBOHYDRATES: 26G; FIBER: 1G; SODIUM: 211MG; PROTEIN: 4G

Wild Rice Hazelnut Bread

PREP TIME IS 10 MINUTES OR LESS

Do not expect a high-rising loaf when you whip up this bread, because it is packed full of fiber and ingredients that create a denser texture. The wild rice has a nutty flavor and looks spectacular when the bread is sliced. A handful of dried cranberries would complement the other ingredients beautifully if you want to experiment.

8 SLICES / 1 POUND

½ cup milk, at 80°F to 90°F

2 teaspoons melted butter, cooled

2 teaspoons honey

⅔ teaspoon salt

⅓ cup cooked wild rice, cooled

⅓ cup whole-wheat flour

⅔ teaspoon caraway seeds

1 cup plus 1 tablespoon white bread flour

1 teaspoon bread machine or instant yeast

⅓ cup chopped hazelnuts

12 SLICES / 1½ POUNDS

¾ cup milk, at 80°F to 90°F

1 tablespoon melted butter, cooled

1 tablespoon honey

1 teaspoon salt

½ cup cooked wild rice, cooled

½ cup whole-wheat flour

1 teaspoon caraway seeds

1⅔ cups white bread flour

1½ teaspoons bread machine or instant yeast

½ cup chopped hazelnuts

16 SLICES / 2 POUNDS

1 cup milk, at 80°F to 90°F

4 teaspoons melted butter, cooled

4 teaspoons honey

1⅓ teaspoons salt

⅔ cup cooked wild rice, cooled

⅔ cup whole-wheat flour

1⅓ teaspoons caraway seeds

2¼ cups white bread flour

2 teaspoons bread machine or instant yeast

⅔ cup chopped hazelnuts

1. Place the ingredients in your bread machine as recommended by the manufacturer.

2. Program the machine for Basic/White bread, select light crust, and press Start.

3. When the loaf is done, remove the bucket from the machine.

4. Let the loaf cool for 5 minutes.

5. Gently shake the bucket to remove the loaf, and turn it out onto a rack to cool.

Cooking tip: Make the wild rice several days in advance, so you are ready to bake this hearty, nutty-tasting bread with no waiting. Cooked wild rice will keep well in the refrigerator, when covered, for up to 4 days.

PER SERVING (1 SLICE): CALORIES: 140; TOTAL FAT: 4G; SATURATED FAT: 1G; CARBOHYDRATES: 23G; FIBER: 2G; SODIUM: 209MG; PROTEIN: 4G

Spinach Feta Bread

PREP TIME IS 10 MINUTES OR LESS

A better name for this loaf might be spanakopita bread, except for the fact that the spinach seems to melt into the dough rather than bake in pockets. The taste is similar to the popular Greek appetizer although a little more subtle. Try serving spinach feta bread with a good quality olive oil for dipping as a starter to a summer meal.

8 SLICES / 1 POUND

⅓ cup cooked chopped spinach, well-drained, cooled

¼ cup water, at 80°F to 90°F

1 small egg, at room temperature

1½ tablespoons melted butter, cooled

¾ tablespoon sugar

¾ teaspoon salt

⅛ teaspoon freshly ground black pepper

2 tablespoons oat bran

1½ cups white bread flour

1⅛ teaspoons bread machine or instant yeast

¼ cup crumbled feta cheese

12 SLICES / 1½ POUNDS

½ cup plus 1 tablespoon cooked chopped spinach, well-drained, cooled

⅓ cup water, at 80°F to 90°F

1 small egg, at room temperature

2¼ tablespoons melted butter, cooled

1⅛ tablespoons sugar

1⅛ teaspoons salt

⅓ teaspoon freshly ground black pepper

⅓ cup oat bran

2¼ cups white bread flour

1⅔ teaspoons bread machine or instant yeast

⅓ cup crumbled feta cheese

16 SLICES / 2 POUNDS

¾ cup cooked chopped spinach, well-drained, cooled

½ cup water, at 80°F to 90°F

1 egg, at room temperature

3 tablespoons melted butter, cooled

1½ tablespoons sugar

1½ teaspoons salt

½ teaspoon freshly ground black pepper

½ cup oat bran

3 cups white bread flour

2¼ teaspoons bread machine or instant yeast

½ cup (2 ounces) crumbled feta cheese

1. Place the ingredients, except the feta cheese, in your bread machine as recommended by the manufacturer.

2. Program the machine for Basic/White bread, select light or medium crust, and press Start.

3. Add the cheese when the machine signals or 5 minutes before the second kneading cycle is finished.

4. When the loaf is done, remove the bucket from the machine.

5. Let the loaf cool for 5 minutes.

6. Gently shake the bucket to remove the loaf, and turn it out onto a rack to cool.

Substitution tip: Thawed frozen spinach or blanched fresh spinach can be used in this recipe with identical results. In order to squeeze all the liquid out, place the greens in the center of a clean cloth, gather the ends together to form a pouch, and twist the pouch until all the water is out.

PER SERVING (1 SLICE): CALORIES: 135; TOTAL FAT: 4G; SATURATED FAT: 2G; CARBOHYDRATES: 21G; FIBER: 1G; SODIUM: 282MG; PROTEIN: 4G

Rum Raisin Bread

PREP TIME IS 10 MINUTES OR LESS

A popular ice cream flavor is the inspiration for this pretty raisin-studded loaf. There is a hefty kick of rum flavor, especially when you bite into a plump, soaked raisin. This bread becomes quite a culinary experience when it is toasted and topped with butter and a sprinkle of brown sugar and cinnamon.

8 SLICES / 1 POUND	12 SLICES / 1½ POUNDS	16 SLICES / 2 POUNDS
2 tablespoons dark rum	3 tablespoons dark rum	¼ cup dark rum
½ cup raisins	¾ cup raisins	1 cup raisins
½ cup plus 2 tablespoons milk, at 80°F to 90°F	1 cup plus 1 tablespoon milk, at 80°F to 90°F	1¼ cups milk, at 80°F to 90°F
1 egg, at room temperature	1 egg, at room temperature	2 eggs, at room temperature
1 tablespoon melted butter, cooled	1½ tablespoons melted butter, cooled	2 tablespoons melted butter, cooled
2 teaspoons light brown sugar	1 tablespoon light brown sugar	4 teaspoons light brown sugar
1 teaspoon salt	1½ teaspoons salt	2 teaspoons salt
½ teaspoon rum flavored extract	¾ teaspoon rum flavored extract	1 teaspoon rum flavored extract
2 cups white bread flour	3 cups white bread flour	4 cups white bread flour
1½ teaspoons bread machine or instant yeast	2¼ teaspoons bread machine or instant yeast	2¾ teaspoons bread machine or instant yeast

1. In a small bowl, stir together the rum and raisins, and let the fruit soak for 30 minutes; drain the raisins.

2. Place the ingredients, except the soaked raisins, in your bread machine as recommended by the manufacturer.

3. Program the machine for Basic/White bread, select light or medium crust, and press Start.

4. Add the raisins when the machine signals or 5 minutes before the second kneading cycle is finished.

5. When the loaf is done, remove the bucket from the machine.

6. Let the loaf cool for 5 minutes.

7. Gently shake the bucket to remove the loaf, and turn it out onto a rack to cool.

Variation tip: Experiment with different types of rum to create the perfect loaf for your palate. Most rum has a distinctive taste, so dark rum, spiced rum, and white rum all produce interesting breads.

PER SERVING (1 SLICE): CALORIES: 184; TOTAL FAT: 3G; SATURATED FAT: 1G; CARBOHYDRATES: 33G; FIBER: 1G; SODIUM: 319MG; PROTEIN: 4G

Bacon Corn Bread

PREP TIME IS 10 MINUTES OR LESS

This savory bread is a perfect snack when you need an energy boost in the afternoon. If you are using a 2-pound machine, take the paddle out of the bucket with tongs after the mixing cycles are complete because this is not a high-rising loaf. If you are not home to do this, you might find that the loaf is hard to cut in the spots where the paddle ended up.

12 TO 16 SLICES / 1½ TO 2 POUNDS

1 cup milk, at room temperature

2 eggs, at room temperature

¼ cup butter, at room temperature

1 cup sugar

2 cups all-purpose flour

1 cup cornmeal

1 tablespoon baking powder

1 teaspoon salt

1 cup cooked crumbled bacon

1. Place the milk, eggs, butter, and sugar in your bread machine.
2. Program the machine for Quick/Rapid bread and press Start.
3. While the wet ingredients are mixing, stir together the flour, cornmeal, baking powder, salt, and bacon in a small bowl.
4. After the first fast mixing is done and the machine signals, add the dry ingredients.
5. When the loaf is done, remove the bucket from the machine.
6. Let the loaf cool for 5 minutes.
7. Gently shake the bucket to remove the loaf, and turn it out onto a rack to cool.

Decoration tip: Sprinkle shredded sharp Cheddar cheese over the batter after the mixing cycles are complete, or top the finished loaf with cheese when it comes out of the bucket piping hot.

PER SERVING (1 SLICE): CALORIES: 250; TOTAL FAT: 7G; SATURATED FAT: 4G; CARBOHYDRATES: 42G; FIBER: 1G; SODIUM: 321MG; PROTEIN: 6G

Oatmeal Coffee Bread

PREP TIME IS 10 MINUTES OR LESS

The alcohol in the small amount of liqueur that flavors this bread bakes out, leaving just a hint of coffee. If you want a nuttier flavor to the bread, toast the oats before you add them to the bucket. Toast them in a nonstick skillet over low heat until they are golden and fragrant.

8 SLICES / 1 POUND	12 SLICES / 1½ POUNDS	16 SLICES / 2 POUNDS
⅔ cup water, at 80°F to 90°F	1 cup water, at 80°F to 90°F	1¼ cup water, at 80°F to 90°F
1 tablespoon Kahlúa or other coffee liqueur	1½ tablespoons Kahlúa or other coffee liqueur	2 tablespoons Kahlúa or other coffee liqueur
2½ tablespoons honey	¼ cup honey	⅓ cup honey
½ teaspoon salt	¾ teaspoon salt	1 teaspoon salt
½ cup quick oats	¾ cup quick oats	1 cup quick oats
1½ cups white bread flour	2¼ cups white bread flour	3 cups white bread flour
1⅛ teaspoons bread machine or instant yeast	1⅔ teaspoons bread machine or instant yeast	2¼ teaspoons bread machine or instant yeast

1. Place the ingredients in your bread machine as recommended by the bread machine manufacturer.
2. Program the machine for Basic/White bread, select light or medium crust, and press Start.
3. When the loaf is done, remove the bucket from the machine.
4. Let the loaf cool for 5 minutes.
5. Gently shake the bucket to remove the loaf, and turn it out onto a rack to cool.

Substitution tip: Other liqueurs, such as Bailey's Original Irish Cream, amaretto, and Irish Mist, would all infuse the bread with an interesting flavor similar to Kahlúa. Make sure your choice is a liqueur with a sweeter taste because the sugar in the Kahlúa feeds the yeast in the bread.

PER SERVING (1 SLICE): CALORIES: 134; TOTAL FAT: 1G; SATURATED FAT: 0G; CARBOHYDRATES: 28G; FIBER: 1G; SODIUM: 149MG; PROTEIN: 3G

Cherry Pistachio Bread

PREP TIME IS 10 MINUTES OR LESS

Whip up a loaf of red- and pastel green-studded bread when you need a pretty platter of tea sandwiches for a special brunch or luncheon. Thinly slice a chilled loaf and spread it with cream cheese or toast the bread and serve it simply with butter and a sprinkle of cinnamon. Pistachios can be quite expensive, so if you want to save a bit of money, shell the pistachios yourself.

8 SLICES / 1 POUND

½ cup water, at 80°F to 90°F

1 egg, at room temperature

2 tablespoons butter, softened

2 tablespoons packed dark brown sugar

¾ teaspoon salt

¼ teaspoon ground nutmeg

Dash allspice

1¾ cups plus 1 tablespoon white bread flour

1 teaspoon bread machine or active dry yeast

½ cup dried cherries

¼ cup chopped unsalted pistachios

12 SLICES / 1½ POUNDS

¾ cup water, at 80°F to 90°F

1 egg, at room temperature

3 tablespoons butter, softened

3 tablespoons packed dark brown sugar

1⅛ teaspoons salt

½ teaspoon ground nutmeg

Dash allspice

2¾ cups white bread flour

1½ teaspoons bread machine or active dry yeast

¾ cup dried cherries

⅓ cup chopped unsalted pistachios

16 SLICES / 2 POUNDS

1 cup plus 2 tablespoons water, at 80°F to 90°F

1 egg, at room temperature

¼ cup butter, softened

¼ cup packed dark brown sugar

1½ teaspoons salt

½ teaspoon ground nutmeg

Dash allspice

3¾ cups white bread flour

2 teaspoons bread machine or active dry yeast

1 cup dried cherries

½ cup chopped unsalted pistachios

1. Place the ingredients, except the cherries and pistachios, in your bread machine as recommended by the manufacturer.
2. Program the machine for Basic/White bread, select light or medium crust, and press Start.
3. Just before the final kneading is over or when the machine signals, add the cherries and pistachios.
4. When the loaf is done, remove the bucket from the machine.
5. Let the loaf cool for 5 minutes.
6. Gently shake the bucket to remove the loaf, and turn it out onto a rack to cool.

Ingredient tip: Dried cherries are sweet with just a hint of sourness and are different than cherry-flavored dried cranberries.

PER SERVING (1 SLICE): CALORIES: 199; TOTAL FAT: 6G; SATURATED FAT: 2G; CARBOHYDRATES: 33G; FIBER: 2G; SODIUM: 248MG; PROTEIN: 5G

Banana Coconut Bread

PREP TIME IS 10 MINUTES OR LESS

Coconut and banana are tropical flavors that typically show up in desserts, smoothies, and frothy cocktails, but they are also delicious in bread. This recipe will be perfect if you are looking for a sweet treat for breakfast to enjoy with a steaming cup of tea or coffee. The loaf freezes beautifully and can be stored in the refrigerator for up to one week.

12 TO 16 SLICES / 1 ½ TO 2 POUNDS

2 ripe bananas, mashed

⅔ cup milk, at 80°F to 90°F

⅓ cup melted butter, cooled

2 eggs, at room temperature

⅔ cup sugar

⅔ teaspoon pure vanilla extract

⅔ teaspoon pure almond extract

1⅔ cups all-purpose flour

⅔ cup shredded sweet coconut

1 teaspoon baking soda

1 teaspoon baking powder

⅓ teaspoon salt

1. Place the bananas, milk, butter, eggs, sugar, vanilla, and almond extract in your bread machine.

2. Program the machine for Quick/Rapid bread and press Start.

3. While the wet ingredients are mixing, stir together the flour, coconut, baking soda, baking powder, and salt in a small bowl.

4. After the first fast mixing is done and the machine signals, add the dry ingredients.

5. When the loaf is done, remove the bucket from the machine.

6. Let the loaf cool for 5 minutes.

7. Gently shake the bucket to remove the loaf, and turn it out onto a rack to cool.

Substitution tip: The same amount of coconut milk can be used in place of cow's milk to intensify the coconut flavor of the bread. Use the type in the carton and not the thick, canned product.

PER SERVING (1 SLICE): CALORIES: 202; TOTAL FAT: 8G; SATURATED FAT: 5G; CARBOHYDRATES: 30G; FIBER: 1G; SODIUM: 226MG; PROTEIN: 4G

Easy Honey Beer Bread

PREP TIME IS 10 MINUTES OR LESS

Many people start their bread-making adventures with simple beer bread because basic recipes have only three or four ingredients—beer, flour, and sugar. Some craft beers still have live yeast, although dormant, in the bottom of the bottles, so they are perfect for bread making. If you are not a fan of the flavor of beer, don't worry. The taste is not apparent after the loaf is baked.

12 TO 16 SLICES / 1½ TO 2 POUNDS

12 ounces beer, at room temperature

⅓ cup melted butter, cooled

¼ cup honey

3 cups all-purpose flour

1 tablespoon baking powder

1 teaspoon salt

¼ teaspoon ground cinnamon

1. Place the beer, butter, and honey in your bread machine.
2. Program the machine for Quick/Rapid bread and press Start.
3. While the wet ingredients are mixing, stir together the flour, baking powder, salt, and cinnamon in a small bowl.
4. After the first fast mixing is done and the machine signals, add the dry ingredients.
5. When the loaf is done, remove the bucket from the machine.
6. Let the loaf cool for 5 minutes.
7. Gently shake the bucket to remove the loaf, and turn it out onto a rack to cool.

Ingredient tip: Beer is a natural ingredient for bread making because it replaces the yeast and liquid in a regular recipe. Use a dark beer for this bread because the flavor of the hops combines beautifully with the honey.

PER SERVING (1 SLICE): CALORIES: 193; TOTAL FAT: 5G; SATURATED FAT: 3G; CARBOHYDRATES: 31G; FIBER: 1G; SODIUM: 233MG; PROTEIN: 3G

Coffee Molasses Bread

PREP TIME IS 10 MINUTES OR LESS

Dark bread can be an acquired taste, especially for kids who may prefer fluffy white bread. Make a peanut butter and honey sandwich with this tasty bread, and they may change their minds. Simply substitute water for the brewed coffee if you want a less-assertive flavor.

8 SLICES / 1 POUND	12 SLICES / 1½ POUNDS	16 SLICES / 2 POUNDS
½ cup brewed coffee, at 80°F to 90°F	¾ cup brewed coffee, at 80°F to 90°F	1 cup brewed coffee, at 80°F to 90°F
½ cup evaporated milk, at 80°F to 90°F	⅓ cup evaporated milk, at 80°F to 90°F	½ cup evaporated milk, at 80°F to 90°F
1 tablespoon melted butter, cooled	1½ tablespoons melted butter, cooled	2 tablespoons melted butter, cooled
1½ tablespoons honey	2¼ tablespoons honey	3 tablespoons honey
½ tablespoon dark molasses	¾ tablespoon dark molasses	1 tablespoon dark molasses
½ tablespoon sugar	¾ tablespoon sugar	1 tablespoon sugar
2 teaspoons unsweetened cocoa powder	1 tablespoon unsweetened cocoa powder	4 teaspoons unsweetened cocoa powder
½ teaspoon salt	¾ teaspoon salt	1 teaspoon salt
1⅛ cups whole-wheat bread flour	1⅔ cups whole-wheat bread flour	2¼ cups whole-wheat bread flour
1⅛ cups white bread flour	1⅔ cups white bread flour	2¼ cups white bread flour
1⅛ teaspoons bread machine or instant yeast	1⅔ teaspoons bread machine or instant yeast	2¼ teaspoons bread machine or instant yeast

1. Place the ingredients in your bread machine as recommended by the manufacturer.
2. Program the machine for Sweet bread and press Start.
3. When the loaf is done, remove the bucket from the machine.
4. Let the loaf cool for 5 minutes.
5. Gently shake the bucket to remove the loaf, and turn it out onto a rack to cool.

Ingredient tip: Be sure to use evaporated milk and not condensed milk. Condensed milk is at least 40 percent sugar, which can affect the ability of the yeast to work in the recipe.

PER SERVING (1 SLICE): CALORIES: 169; TOTAL FAT: 2G; SATURATED FAT: 1G; CARBOHYDRATES: 33G; FIBER: 1G; SODIUM: 167MG; PROTEIN: 4G

Pear Sweet Potato Bread

PREP TIME IS 10 MINUTES OR LESS

The best way to cook the sweet potato for this bread is to bake it in the skin, in a hot oven until it is tender and soft. The flavor of the potato will be intensely sweet. Simply scoop the cooked flesh out of the skin and mash it until it is fluffy.

8 SLICES / 1 POUND

⅓ cup plus 1 tablespoon milk, at 80°F to 90°F

⅓ cup shredded peeled pear

⅓ cup mashed cooked sweet potato, cooled

1½ tablespoons melted butter, cooled

1½ tablespoons sugar

¾ teaspoon salt

¼ teaspoon ground cinnamon

¼ teaspoon ground nutmeg

⅛ teaspoon ground ginger

2 cups white bread flour

⅔ teaspoons bread machine or instant yeast

12 SLICES / 1½ POUNDS

½ cup plus 1 tablespoon milk, at 80°F to 90°F

½ cup shredded peeled pear

½ cup mashed cooked sweet potato, cooled

2¼ tablespoons melted butter, cooled

2¼ tablespoons sugar

1 teaspoon salt

⅓ teaspoon ground cinnamon

⅓ teaspoon ground nutmeg

⅛ teaspoon ground ginger

3 cups white bread flour

1 teaspoon bread machine or instant yeast

16 SLICES / 2 POUNDS

¾ cup milk, at 80°F to 90°F

⅔ cup shredded peeled pear

⅔ cup mashed cooked sweet potato, cooled

3 tablespoons melted butter, cooled

3 tablespoons sugar

1½ teaspoons salt

½ teaspoon ground cinnamon

½ teaspoon ground nutmeg

¼ teaspoon ground ginger

3¾ cups white bread flour

1¼ teaspoons bread machine or instant yeast

1. Place the ingredients in your bread machine as recommended by the manufacturer.

2. Program the machine for Sweet bread and press Start.

3. When the loaf is done, remove the bucket from the machine.

4. Let the loaf cool for 5 minutes.

5. Gently shake the bucket to remove the loaf, and turn it out onto a rack to cool.

Substitution tip: Yams are not the same as sweet potatoes, but they can also be used in this recipe. The taste will be similar, but yams are starchier with white flesh, so the bread will not be tinted orange.

PER SERVING (1 SLICE): CALORIES: 163; TOTAL FAT: 3G; SATURATED FAT: 2G; CARBOHYDRATES: 31G; FIBER: 2G; SODIUM: 218MG; PROTEIN: 4G

—Chapter Ten—

HOLIDAY BREADS

Panettone Bread

PREP TIME IS 10 MINUTES OR LESS

Holiday time would not be the same in many countries without this sweet, fruit-studded favorite. Traditional panettone is made in a cupola shape, but the familiar bread machine loaf shape works just fine. This pretty bread has long culinary roots back to the Roman Empire when leavened bread was sweetened with honey. Serve it sliced accompanied by coffee or a sweet, hot drink.

8 SLICES / 1 POUND

½ cup milk, at 80°F to 90°F

3 tablespoons melted butter, cooled

1 egg, at room temperature

1⅓ teaspoons pure vanilla extract

4 teaspoons sugar

1 teaspoon salt

2 cups plus 2 tablespoons white bread flour

1½ teaspoons bread machine or instant yeast

3 tablespoons candied lemon peel

3 tablespoons candied orange peel

12 SLICES / 1½ POUNDS

¾ cup milk, at 80°F to 90°F

¼ cup melted butter, cooled

2 eggs, at room temperature

2 teaspoons pure vanilla extract

2 tablespoons sugar

1½ teaspoons salt

3¼ cups white bread flour

2 teaspoons bread machine or instant yeast

¼ cup candied lemon peel

¼ cup candied orange peel

16 SLICES / 2 POUNDS

1 cup milk, at 80°F to 90°F

5 tablespoons melted butter, cooled

3 eggs, at room temperature

2 teaspoons pure vanilla extract

2⅔ tablespoons sugar

2 teaspoons salt

4⅓ cups white bread flour

2¼ teaspoons bread machine or instant yeast

⅓ cup candied lemon peel

⅓ cup candied orange peel

1. Place the ingredients, except the candied fruit peel, in your bread machine as recommended by the manufacturer.
2. Program the machine for Sweet bread, select light or medium crust, and press Start.
3. When the machine signals, add the peel, or place in the nut/raisin hopper and let the machine add the peel automatically.
4. When the loaf is done, remove the bucket from the machine.
5. Let the loaf cool for 5 minutes.
6. Gently shake the bucket to remove the loaf, and turn it out onto a rack to cool.

Variation tip: Any type of candied or dried fruit can be used in the bread, such as cherries, lime peel, raisins, and even candied papaya. Keep the quantity the same so the bread rises well.

PER SERVING (1 SLICE): CALORIES: 191; TOTAL FAT: 5G; SATURATED FAT: 3G; CARBOHYDRATES: 30G; FIBER: 1G; SODIUM: 338MG; PROTEIN: 5G

White Chocolate Cranberry Bread

PREP TIME IS 10 MINUTES OR LESS

The sweetness of the white chocolate is balanced perfectly by the tart cranberries in this pretty bread. Although white chocolate is not considered to be a true chocolate by most culinary experts, there is always a place in our hearts for its candy–like flavor. Look for a pale ivory color rather than pure white to ensure your white chocolate has cocoa butter in it rather than vegetable oil.

8 SLICES / 1 POUND	12 SLICES / 1½ POUNDS	16 SLICES / 2 POUNDS
½ cup plus 1 tablespoon milk, at 80°F to 90°F	¾ cup plus 2 tablespoons milk, at 80°F to 90°F	1 cup plus 3 tablespoons milk, at 80°F to 90°F
1 egg, at room temperature	1 egg, at room temperature	1 egg, at room temperature
1 tablespoon melted butter, cooled	1½ tablespoons melted butter, cooled	2 tablespoons melted butter, cooled
⅔ teaspoon pure vanilla extract	1 teaspoon pure vanilla extract	1½ teaspoons pure vanilla extract
4 teaspoons sugar	2 tablespoons sugar	2⅔ tablespoons sugar
½ teaspoon salt	¾ teaspoon salt	1 teaspoon salt
2 cups white bread flour	3 cups white bread flour	4 cups white bread flour
¾ teaspoon bread machine or instant yeast	1 teaspoon bread machine or instant yeast	1⅓ teaspoons bread machine or instant yeast
⅓ cup white chocolate chips	½ cup white chocolate chips	⅔ cup white chocolate chips
¼ cup sweetened dried cranberries	⅓ cup sweetened dried cranberries	½ cup sweetened dried cranberries

1. Place the ingredients, except the chocolate chips and cranberries, in your bread machine as recommended by the manufacturer.
2. Program the machine for Basic/White bread, select light or medium crust, and press Start.
3. Add the white chocolate chips and cranberries when the machine signals or 5 minutes before the last knead cycle ends.
4. When the loaf is done, remove the bucket from the machine.
5. Let the loaf cool for 5 minutes.
6. Gently shake the bucket to remove the loaf, and turn it out onto a rack to cool.

Decoration tip: If you don't plan to toast this bread, drizzle melted white chocolate over the top of the cooled loaf. The simplest method to use is dipping a fork in the melted chocolate and letting it stream from the tines in a random pattern.

PER SERVING (1 SLICE): CALORIES: 201; TOTAL FAT: 5G; SATURATED FAT: 3G; CARBOHYDRATES: 34G; FIBER: 1G; SODIUM: 179MG; PROTEIN: 5G

Eggnog Bread

PREP TIME IS 10 MINUTES OR LESS

Eggnog is a favorite beverage during the holidays, and it can be bought in cartons at any local grocery store. This rich and creamy drink creates a rich and tender egg bread with a nutmeg flavor, enhanced by the other spices in the recipe. Make sure you purchase full-fat eggnog, not the lower fat version.

8 SLICES / 1 POUND	12 SLICES / 1 ½ POUNDS	16 SLICES / 2 POUNDS
¾ cup eggnog, at 80°F to 90°F	1 cup plus 2 tablespoons eggnog, at 80°F to 90°F	1½ cups eggnog, at 80°F to 90°F
¾ tablespoon melted butter, cooled	1⅛ tablespoons melted butter, cooled	1½ tablespoons melted butter, cooled
1 tablespoon sugar	1½ tablespoons sugar	2 tablespoons sugar
⅔ teaspoon salt	1 teaspoon salt	1¼ teaspoons salt
¼ teaspoon ground cinnamon	⅓ teaspoon ground cinnamon	½ teaspoon ground cinnamon
¼ teaspoon ground nutmeg	⅓ teaspoon ground nutmeg	½ teaspoon ground nutmeg
2 cups white bread flour	3 cups white bread flour	4 cups white bread flour
¾ teaspoon bread machine or instant yeast	1⅓ teaspoons bread machine or instant yeast	1¾ teaspoons bread machine or instant yeast

1. Place the ingredients in your bread machine as recommended by the manufacturer.

2. Program the machine for Basic/White bread, select light or medium crust, and press Start.

3. When the loaf is done, remove the bucket from the machine.

4. Let the loaf cool for 5 minutes.

5. Gently shake the bucket to remove the loaf, and turn it out onto a rack to cool.

Ingredient tip: You will have leftover eggnog after making this bread, so why not try it in a favorite cake recipe in place of regular milk? This delightful, seasonal beverage even makes cake from a boxed mix taste incredible.

PER SERVING (1 SLICE): CALORIES: 162; TOTAL FAT: 3G; SATURATED FAT: 2G; CARBOHYDRATES: 29G; FIBER: 1G; SODIUM: 214MG; PROTEIN: 4G

Whole-Wheat Challah

PREP TIME IS 10 MINUTES OR LESS

Challah has a long history as the Shabbat and holiday bread of Jewish people world-wide, so it is important to create bread that lives up to this important purpose. There are many different types of challah, and this recipe features a whole-wheat version. The rectangular shape of the bread machine will produce a shape that is not tradi-tional, but the taste will still be amazing.

8 SLICES / 1 POUND	12 SLICES / 1½ POUNDS	16 SLICES / 2 POUNDS
½ cup water, at 80°F to 90°F	¾ cup water, at 80°F to 90°F	1 cup water, at 80°F to 90°F
¼ cup melted butter, cooled	⅓ cup melted butter, cooled	½ cup melted butter, cooled
1 egg, at room temperature	2 eggs, at room temperature	2 eggs, at room temperature
1 teaspoon salt	1½ teaspoons salt	2 teaspoons salt
2 tablespoons sugar	3 tablespoons sugar	¼ cup sugar
¾ cup whole-wheat flour	1 cup whole-wheat flour	1½ cups whole-wheat flour
1¼ cups white bread flour	2 cups white bread flour	2½ cups white bread flour
1⅛ teaspoons bread machine or instant yeast	1⅔ teaspoons bread machine or instant yeast	2¼ teaspoons bread machine or instant yeast

1. Place the ingredients in your bread machine as recommended by the manufacturer.
2. Program the machine for Basic/White bread, select light or medium crust, and press Start.
3. When the loaf is done, remove the bucket from the machine.
4. Let the loaf cool for 5 minutes.
5. Gently shake the bucket to remove the loaf, and turn it out onto a rack to cool.

Cooking tip: If you want to create a traditional challah braid, remove the dough after it has been kneaded by the bread machine, let it rise in a bowl, punch it down, and form a pretty braid with the dough. Let it rise again on a baking sheet and then bake the bread for 50 minutes in a traditional oven preheated to 350°F.

PER SERVING (1 SLICE): CALORIES: 183; TOTAL FAT: 6G; SATURATED FAT: 4G; CARBOHYDRATES: 27G; FIBER: 1G; SODIUM: 339MG; PROTEIN: 5G

Portuguese Sweet Bread

PREP TIME IS 10 MINUTES OR LESS

Easter and Christmas are the traditional holidays for this simple milk bread. Often, a hardboiled egg is baked right into the loaf. Even if you don't add a hardboiled egg, the taste and texture will still come out perfect from your bread machine. Try a slice warm topped with a little bit of sweet butter.

8 SLICES / 1 POUND	12 SLICES / 1 ½ POUNDS	16 SLICES / 2 POUNDS
⅔ cup milk, at 80°F to 90°F	1 cup milk, at 80°F to 90°F	1⅓ cup milk, at 80°F to 90°F
1 egg, at room temperature	1 egg, at room temperature	1 egg, at room temperature
4 teaspoons butter, softened	2 tablespoons butter, softened	2⅔ tablespoons butter, softened
⅓ cup sugar	½ cup sugar	⅔ cup sugar
⅔ teaspoon salt	1 teaspoon salt	1⅓ teaspoons salt
2 cups white bread flour	3 cups white bread flour	4 cups white bread flour
1½ teaspoons bread machine or instant yeast	2¼ teaspoons bread machine or instant yeast	2¼ teaspoons bread machine or instant yeast

1. Place the ingredients in your bread machine as recommended by the manufacturer.
2. Program the machine for Sweet bread and press Start.
3. When the loaf is done, remove the bucket from the machine.
4. Let the loaf cool for 5 minutes.
5. Gently shake the bucket to remove the loaf, and turn it out onto a rack to cool.

Variation tip: Some recipes for Portuguese sweet bread call for lemon or orange zest, rum, whiskey, currants, or raisins. These ingredients can be added to your bread machine as well. If you add a liquid, take out the same amount from the milk. If you add dried fruit, add it when the machine signals or just before the second kneading cycle ends.

PER SERVING (1 SLICE): CALORIES: 180; TOTAL FAT: 3G; SATURATED FAT: 2G; CARBOHYDRATES: 34G; FIBER: 1G; SODIUM: 224MG; PROTEIN: 5G

Pecan Maple Bread

PREP TIME IS 10 MINUTES OR LESS

If you have a 1-pound machine, you can still make this sweet, nutty loaf as long as you have an "add time" feature. Many bread machines allow baking time to be extended in intervals, so you can bake loaves longer when they are not quite done. Insert a knife into the bread just before the cycle is done, and add time if the batter is still wet.

16 SLICES / 2 POUNDS

1½ cups (3 sticks) butter, at room temperature

4 eggs, at room temperature

⅔ cup maple syrup

⅔ cup sugar

3 cups all-purpose flour

1 cup chopped pecans

2 teaspoons baking powder

½ teaspoon salt

1. Place the butter, eggs, maple syrup, and sugar in your bread machine.
2. Program the machine for Quick/Rapid bread and press Start.
3. While the wet ingredients are mixing, stir together the flour, pecans, baking powder, and salt in a small bowl.
4. After the first fast mixing is done and the machine signals, add the dry ingredients.
5. When the loaf is done, remove the bucket from the machine.
6. Let the loaf cool for 5 minutes.
7. Gently shake the bucket to remove the loaf, and turn it out onto a rack to cool.

Decoration tip: Sprinkle extra pecans on top of the batter after the mixing cycle is complete, so the finished loaf is studded with nuts.

PER SERVING (1 SLICE): CALORIES: 340; TOTAL FAT: 20G; SATURATED FAT: 11G; CARBOHYDRATES: 36G; FIBER: 1G; SODIUM: 216MG; PROTEIN: 5G

Nana's Gingerbread

PREP TIME IS 10 MINUTES OR LESS

This yeast bread has the aroma of gingerbread cookies and just enough sugar to be eaten without any embellishments. It would also be an inspired choice if you want to make a bread pudding for the holidays. Simply cut the chilled loaf into thick chunks and add the pieces to the other pudding ingredients with the crust still on.

8 SLICES / 1 POUND

⅔ cup buttermilk, at 80°F to 90°F

1 egg, at room temperature

2⅔ tablespoons dark molasses

2 teaspoons melted butter, cooled

2 tablespoons sugar

1 teaspoon salt

1 teaspoon ground ginger

⅔ teaspoon ground cinnamon

⅓ teaspoon ground nutmeg

⅛ teaspoon ground cloves

2⅓ cups white bread flour

1⅓ teaspoons bread machine or active dry yeast

12 SLICES / 1 ½ POUNDS

1 cup buttermilk, at 80°F to 90°F

1 egg, at room temperature

¼ cup dark molasses

1 tablespoon melted butter, cooled

3 tablespoons sugar

1½ teaspoons salt

1½ teaspoons ground ginger

1 teaspoon ground cinnamon

½ teaspoon ground nutmeg

¼ teaspoon ground cloves

3½ cups white bread flour

2 teaspoons bread machine or active dry yeast

16 SLICES / 2 POUNDS

1⅓ cup buttermilk, at 80°F to 90°F

1 egg, at room temperature

⅓ cup dark molasses

4 teaspoons melted butter, cooled

¼ cup sugar

2 teaspoons salt

2 teaspoons ground ginger

1¼ teaspoons ground cinnamon

⅔ teaspoon ground nutmeg

⅓ teaspoon ground cloves

4¼ cups white bread flour

2¼ teaspoons bread machine or active dry yeast

1. Place the ingredients in your bread machine as recommended by the manufacturer.
2. Program the machine for Sweet bread and press Start.
3. When the loaf is done, remove the bucket from the machine.
4. Let the loaf cool for 5 minutes.
5. Gently shake the bucket to remove the loaf, and turn it out onto a rack to cool.

"Did You Know?" Back when churning fresh milk made butter, buttermilk was the liquid left over after the butter was removed from the churn. Today, store-bought versions of this low-fat dairy product are made by adding a bacteria culture to sweet milk and letting the liquid ferment.

PER SERVING (1 SLICE): CALORIES: 190; TOTAL FAT: 2G; SATURATED FAT: 1G; CARBOHYDRATES: 38G; FIBER: 1G; SODIUM: 329MG; PROTEIN: 5G

Bread Machine Brioche

PREP TIME IS 10 MINUTES OR LESS

You will have to do a little more work in order to make this bread soft, light, and intensely buttery. Brioche is traditional French bread that is a cross between traditional bread and pastry. True brioche is often served as dessert because of its rich taste.

8 SLICES / 1 POUND	12 SLICES / 1½ POUNDS	16 SLICES / 2 POUNDS
¼ cup plus 2 tablespoons milk, at 80°F to 90°F	½ cup plus 1 tablespoon milk, at 80°F to 90°F	¾ cup milk, at 80°F to 90°F
2 eggs, at room temperature	3 eggs, at room temperature	4 eggs, at room temperature
4 teaspoons sugar	2 tablespoons sugar	2⅔ tablespoons sugar
½ teaspoon salt	¾ teaspoon salt	1 teaspoon salt
2 cups white bread flour	3 cups white bread flour	4 cups white bread flour
1 teaspoon bread machine or instant yeast	1½ teaspoons bread machine or instant yeast	2 teaspoons bread machine or instant yeast
⅓ cup butter, softened	½ cup (1 stick) butter, softened	½ cup (1 stick) plus 3⅓ tablespoons butter, softened

1. Place the ingredients in your bread machine as recommended by the manufacturer.
2. Program the machine for Basic/White bread, select light crust, and press Start.
3. Cut the butter into tablespoon-sized pieces.
4. About 10 minutes before the end of your first kneading cycle, begin adding the butter, 1 tablespoon each minute.
5. When the loaf is done, remove the bucket from the machine.
6. Let the loaf cool for 5 minutes.
7. Gently shake the bucket to remove the loaf, and turn it out onto a rack to cool.

Cooking tip: The temperature of the softened butter is crucial for perfect brioche texture. If it is too hard, the dough won't have that meltingly soft texture. If your butter is hard at all, wait a bit before starting to make this bread.

PER SERVING (1 SLICE): CALORIES: 214; TOTAL FAT: 10G; SATURATED FAT: 5G; CARBOHYDRATES: 27G; FIBER: 1G; SODIUM: 226MG; PROTEIN: 6G

Traditional Paska

PREP TIME IS 10 MINUTES OR LESS

Paska is a classic Ukrainian Easter bread that is traditionally iced on top like a cake or topped with a braided dough cross. This is a simple bread made with flour, eggs, sugar, and butter, but the lemon zest in this variation adds a lovely flavor. Paska can be served as a dessert, but it also makes an incredible French toast.

8 SLICES / 1 POUND	12 SLICES / 1½ POUNDS	16 SLICES / 2 POUNDS
⅓ cup milk, at 80°F to 90°F	¾ cup milk, at 80°F to 90°F	1 cup milk, at 80°F to 90°F
2 eggs, at room temperature	2 eggs, at room temperature	2 eggs, at room temperature
4 teaspoons butter, melted and cooled	2 tablespoons butter, melted and cooled	2⅔ tablespoons butter, melted and cooled
2⅔ tablespoons sugar	¼ cup sugar	⅓ cup sugar
⅔ teaspoon salt	1 teaspoon salt	1 teaspoon salt
1⅓ teaspoons lemon zest	2 teaspoons lemon zest	2⅓ teaspoons lemon zest
2 cups white bread flour	3 cups white bread flour	4 cups white bread flour
1⅓ teaspoons bread machine or instant yeast	2 teaspoons bread machine or instant yeast	2¼ teaspoons bread machine or instant yeast

1. Place the ingredients in your bread machine as recommended by the manufacturer.
2. Program the machine for Basic/White bread, select light or medium crust, and press Start.
3. When the loaf is done, remove the bucket from the machine.
4. Let the loaf cool for 5 minutes.
5. Gently shake the bucket to remove the loaf, and turn it out onto a rack to cool.

"Did You Know?" From adding a refreshing zing to your water to marinating your fish to perfection, lemons serve a wide range of culinary functions. Lemon peels contain as much as 5 to 10 times more vitamins than the lemon juice itself, which include vitamin C, vitamin A, beta carotene, and folate. They're also full of fiber.

PER SERVING (1 SLICE): CALORIES: 168; TOTAL FAT: 3G; SATURATED FAT: 2G; CARBOHYDRATES: 29G; FIBER: 1G; SODIUM: 227MG; PROTEIN: 5G

Raisin and Nut Paska

PREP TIME IS 10 MINUTES OR LESS

Paska is a sweet fruit and nut bread made at Easter time in Eastern Europe. In this version, the flavor of almonds infuse every bite of this loaf. You can also try pecans, pistachios, or hazelnuts instead of the almonds.

8 SLICES / 1 POUND	12 SLICES / 1 ½ POUNDS	16 SLICES / 2 POUNDS
⅓ cup milk, at 80°F to 90°F	¾ cup milk, at 80°F to 90°F	1 cup milk, at 80°F to 90°F
2 eggs, at room temperature	2 eggs, at room temperature	2 eggs, at room temperature
4 teaspoons butter, melted and cooled	2 tablespoons butter, melted and cooled	2⅔ tablespoons butter, melted and cooled
2⅔ tablespoons sugar	¼ cup sugar	⅓ cup sugar
⅔ teaspoon salt	1 teaspoon salt	1 teaspoon salt
1⅓ teaspoons lemon zest	2 teaspoons lemon zest	2⅓ teaspoons lemon zest
2 cups white bread flour	3 cups white bread flour	4 cups white bread flour
1⅓ teaspoons bread machine or instant yeast	2 teaspoons bread machine or instant yeast	2¼ teaspoons bread machine or instant yeast
¼ cup slivered almonds	⅓ cup slivered almonds	½ cup slivered almonds
¼ cup golden raisins	⅓ cup golden raisins	½ cup golden raisins

1. Place the ingredients, except the almonds and raisins, in your bread machine as recommended by the manufacturer.
2. Program the machine for Basic/White bread, select light or medium crust, and press Start.
3. Add the almonds and raisins when the machine signals or 5 minutes before the second kneading cycle is finished.
4. When the loaf is done, remove the bucket from the machine.
5. Let the loaf cool for 5 minutes.
6. Gently shake the bucket to remove the loaf, and turn it out onto a rack to cool.

Decoration tip: Traditional paska has very elaborate designs on top of the bread that are created with dough and washed with egg. After this loaf comes out of the bucket, brush it with melted butter to create a similar sheen.

PER SERVING (1 SLICE): CALORIES: 195; TOTAL FAT: 5G; SATURATED FAT: 2G; CARBOHYDRATES: 33G; FIBER: 2G; SODIUM: 228MG; PROTEIN: 6G

Honey Cake

PREP TIME IS 10 MINUTES OR LESS

Honey cake is served for the Jewish New Year, or Rosh Hashanah, and it is meant to symbolize the sweetness in the year to come. Although called a honey cake, this rich and nicely spiced loaf is reminiscent of spekulaas cookies (or Dutch windmill cookies). The cake gets more moist and the flavors intensify after a few days, but it's also delicious to eat right away.

12 TO 16 SLICES / 1½ TO 2 POUNDS

⅓ cup brewed coffee, cooled to room temperature

½ cup (1 stick) butter, melted and cooled

½ cup honey

¾ cup sugar

¼ cup dark brown sugar

2 eggs, at room temperature

2 tablespoons whiskey

¼ cup freshly squeezed orange juice, at room temperature

1 teaspoon pure vanilla extract

2 cups all-purpose flour

½ tablespoon baking powder

½ tablespoon ground cinnamon

½ teaspoon baking soda

¼ teaspoon ground allspice

¼ teaspoon salt

¼ teaspoon ground cloves

1. Place the coffee, butter, honey, sugar, brown sugar, eggs, whiskey, orange juice, and vanilla in your bread machine.

2. Program the machine for Quick/Rapid bread and press Start.

3. While the wet ingredients are mixing, stir together the flour, baking powder, cinnamon, baking soda, allspice, salt, and cloves in a small bowl.

4. After the first fast mixing is done and the machine signals, add the dry ingredients.

5. When the loaf is done, remove the bucket from the machine.

6. Let the loaf cool for 5 minutes.

7. Gently shake the bucket to remove the loaf, and turn it out onto a rack to cool.

Ingredient tip: If you wish to have an even richer cake, use half a vanilla bean instead of the extract in the recipe. Cut the bean open lengthwise, and use the tip of a paring knife to scrape the seeds into the wet ingredients in the bucket.

PER SERVING (1 SLICE): CALORIES: 268; TOTAL FAT: 9G; SATURATED FAT: 5G; CARBOHYDRATES: 44G; FIBER: 1G; SODIUM: 171MG; PROTEIN: 3G

Christmas Fruit Bread

PREP TIME IS 10 MINUTES OR LESS

This is definitely not the dreaded fruitcake that your distant aunt sends every holiday. Those loaves are often dense enough to be paperweights and too packed with candied or dried fruit to allow you to taste anything else. This light yeast bread has a hint of the traditional flavor with a delicate scattering of fruit in the center.

8 SLICES / 1 POUND

¾ cup plus 1 tablespoon milk, at 80°F to 90°F

2⅔ tablespoons melted butter, cooled

⅓ teaspoon pure vanilla extract

⅛ teaspoon pure almond extract

2 tablespoons light brown sugar

⅔ teaspoon salt

1 teaspoon ground cinnamon

2 cups white bread flour

⅔ teaspoon bread machine or instant yeast

⅓ cup dried mixed fruit

⅓ cup golden raisins

12 SLICES / 1½ POUNDS

1¼ cups milk, at 80°F to 90°F

¼ cup melted butter, cooled

½ teaspoon pure vanilla extract

¼ teaspoon pure almond extract

3 tablespoons light brown sugar

1 teaspoon salt

2 teaspoons ground cinnamon

3 cups white bread flour

1 teaspoon bread machine or instant yeast

½ cup dried mixed fruit

½ cup golden raisins

16 SLICES / 2 POUNDS

1⅔ cups milk, at 80°F to 90°F

⅓ cup melted butter, cooled

⅔ teaspoon pure vanilla extract

¼ teaspoon pure almond extract

⅓ cup light brown sugar

1⅓ teaspoons salt

2 teaspoons ground cinnamon

4 cups white bread flour

1⅔ teaspoons bread machine or instant yeast

⅔ cup dried mixed fruit

⅔ cup golden raisins

1. Place the ingredients, except the dried fruit and raisins, in your bread machine as recommended by the manufacturer.
2. Program the machine for Basic/White bread, select light or medium crust, and press Start.
3. Add the dried fruit and raisins when the machine signals or 5 minutes before the second kneading cycle is finished.
4. When the loaf is done, remove the bucket from the machine.
5. Let the loaf cool for 5 minutes.
6. Gently shake the bucket to remove the loaf, and turn it out onto a rack to cool.

Variation tip: There are no definitive rules when it comes to the dried mixed fruit in Christmas cake, so pick your favorite types. Candied cherries, orange or lemon peel, currants, and dried blueberries are all delicious. Use the same amount as is called for in the recipe, and toss them in a couple tablespoons of flour (taken out of the flour measurement) so the fruit doesn't stick together.

PER SERVING (1 SLICE): CALORIES: 200; TOTAL FAT: 5G; SATURATED FAT: 3G; CARBOHYDRATES: 35G; FIBER: 2G; SODIUM: 235MG; PROTEIN: 5G

Stollen

PREP TIME IS 10 MINUTES OR LESS

Stollen is traditional Christmas bread with a history that dates back to the 14th century. The original bread was created without butter, fruit, or nuts, so it certainly did not taste as delicious as it does today. Candied lemon or orange peel would make a great addition to the bread, as well.

8 SLICES / 1 POUND

⅔ cup milk, at 80°F to 90°F

1 egg, at room temperature

1 tablespoon butter, melted and cooled

1½ tablespoons light brown sugar

⅛ teaspoon ground cinnamon

2 cups white bread flour, divided

¾ teaspoons bread machine or instant yeast

⅓ cup red and green candied cherries

¼ cup chopped almonds

¼ cup raisins

12 SLICES / 1½ POUNDS

¾ cup milk, at 80°F to 90°F

1 egg, at room temperature

1½ tablespoons butter, melted and cooled

2¼ tablespoons light brown sugar

⅛ teaspoon ground cinnamon

3 cups white bread flour, divided

1⅛ teaspoons bread machine or instant yeast

½ cup red and green candied cherries

⅓ cup chopped almonds

⅓ cup raisins

16 SLICES / 2 POUNDS

1 cup plus 1 tablespoon milk, at 80°F to 90°F

1 egg, at room temperature

2 tablespoons butter, melted and cooled

3 tablespoons light brown sugar

⅛ teaspoon ground cinnamon

4 cups white bread flour, divided

1½ teaspoons bread machine or instant yeast

⅔ cup red and green candied cherries

½ cup chopped almonds

½ cup raisins

1. Place the ingredients, except the candied fruit, nuts, raisins, and ¼ cup of the flour, in your bread machine as recommended by the manufacturer.

2. Program the machine for Basic/White bread, select light or medium crust, and press Start.

3. In a small bowl, stir together the candied cherries, almonds, raisins, and ¼ cup of flour.

4. Add the fruit and nut mixture when the machine signals or 5 minutes before the second kneading cycle is finished.

5. When the loaf is done, remove the bucket from the machine.

6. Let the loaf cool for 5 minutes.

7. Gently shake the bucket to remove the loaf, and turn it out onto a rack to cool.

Cooking tip: Do not skip the step of tossing the candied cherries, raisins, and nuts in the flour, or you might end up with a loaf that has a lump of fruit in it. Candied cherries are very sticky, so they need a dusting of flour to disperse well in the dough.

PER SERVING (1 SLICE): CALORIES: 184; TOTAL FAT: 4G; SATURATED FAT: 1G; CARBOHYDRATES: 33G; FIBER: 2G; SODIUM: 25MG; PROTEIN: 5G

Julekake

PREP TIME IS 10 MINUTES OR LESS

Julecake, or "Yule Bread," is a rich, heavily spiced bread traditionally baked in a cake pan and served at Christmas in many Scandinavian countries. As the name would indicate, it is more like a cake than a bread. It is best served warm with butter, but you could also put a sweet confectioner's sugar icing on the top before slicing.

8 SLICES / 1 POUND

⅔ cup milk, at 80°F to 90°F

1 egg, at room temperature

⅓ cup butter, melted and cooled

2⅔ tablespoons honey

⅓ teaspoon salt

⅓ teaspoon ground cardamom

¼ teaspoon ground cinnamon

2¼ cups white bread flour, plus 1 tablespoon

1½ teaspoons bread machine or instant yeast

⅓ cup golden raisins

⅓ cup candied citrus fruit

2⅔ tablespoons candied cherries

12 SLICES / 1½ POUNDS

1 cup milk, at 80°F to 90°F

1 egg, at room temperature

½ cup (1 stick) butter, melted and cooled

¼ cup honey

½ teaspoon salt

½ teaspoon ground cardamom

¼ teaspoon ground cinnamon

3⅓ cups white bread flour, plus 1 tablespoon

2¼ teaspoons bread machine or instant yeast

½ cup golden raisins

½ cup candied citrus fruit

¼ cup candied cherries

16 SLICES / 2 POUNDS

1⅓ cup milk, at 80°F to 90°F

1 egg, at room temperature

⅔ cup butter, melted and cooled

5 tablespoons honey

⅔ teaspoon salt

⅔ teaspoon ground cardamom

¼ teaspoon ground cinnamon

4⅓ cups white bread flour, plus 1 tablespoon

1 tablespoon bread machine or instant yeast

⅔ cup golden raisins

⅔ cup candied citrus fruit

5 tablespoons candied cherries

1. Place the ingredients, except the raisins, candied citrus fruit, and 1 tablespoon of flour, in your bread machine as recommended by the manufacturer.

2. Program the machine for Basic/White bread, select light or medium crust, and press Start.

3. Toss the raisins, candied citrus fruit, and 1 tablespoon of flour together in a small bowl.

4. Add the raisins, candied citrus fruit, and flour when the machine signals or 5 minutes before the second kneading cycle is finished.

5. When the loaf is done, remove the bucket from the machine.

6. Let the loaf cool for 5 minutes.

7. Gently shake the bucket to remove the loaf, and turn it out onto a rack to cool.

"Did You Know?" Candied cherries are also called glacé cherries and are French in origin. Authentic glacé cherries are produced using time-honored methods designed to preserve the flavor of the fruit.

PER SERVING (1 SLICE): CALORIES: 256; TOTAL FAT: 9G; SATURATED FAT: 6G; CARBOHYDRATES: 40G; FIBER: 2G; SODIUM: 168MG; PROTEIN: 5G

Spiked Eggnog Bread

PREP TIME IS 10 MINUTES OR LESS

Eggnog is a perfect ingredient for holiday quick breads because it is made with milk, egg yolks, and spices—all common ingredients in baking. You can find reference to this popular beverage as far back as the 13th century, when it was called "posset." The supermarket version of the drink is fine for this recipe, but for a real treat, try homemade eggnog.

12 TO 16 SLICES / 1½ TO 2 POUNDS

1 cup eggnog, at room temperature

1 cup sugar

2 eggs, at room temperature

½ cup (1 stick) butter, at room temperature

1 tablespoon dark rum

1½ teaspoons pure vanilla extract

½ teaspoon rum extract

2¼ cups all-purpose flour

2 teaspoons baking powder

¼ teaspoon ground cinnamon

½ teaspoon ground nutmeg

½ teaspoon salt

1. Place the eggnog, sugar, eggs, butter, rum, vanilla, and rum extract in your bread machine.

2. Program the machine for Quick/Rapid bread and press Start.

3. While the wet ingredients are mixing, stir together the flour, baking powder, cinnamon, nutmeg, and salt in a small bowl.

4. After the first fast mixing is done and the machine signals, add the dry ingredients.

5. When the loaf is done, remove the bucket from the machine.

6. Let the loaf cool for 5 minutes.

7. Gently shake the bucket to remove the loaf, and turn it out onto a rack to cool.

Decoration tip: Whip together a rum-spiked eggnog glaze to drizzle over this special loaf after it is cooled. Stir together 3 tablespoons of eggnog, a generous splash of rum extract, and about ¾ cup confectioner's sugar for a thick, sugary icing.

PER SERVING (1 SLICE): CALORIES: 262; TOTAL FAT: 10G; SATURATED FAT: 6G; CARBOHYDRATES: 38G; FIBER: 1G; SODIUM: 176MG; PROTEIN: 4G

Hot Buttered Rum Bread

PREP TIME IS 10 MINUTES OR LESS

A generous scoop of raisins or pecans could enhance this already outstanding loaf if you want a little extra boost. The rum extract can be replaced with real rum, but the flavor will be less assertive. Try almond butter and slices of banana as a sandwich filling.

8 SLICES / 1 POUND

½ cup minus 1 tablespoon water, at 80°F to 90°F

1 egg, at room temperature

2 tablespoons butter, melted and cooled

2 tablespoons sugar

2 teaspoons rum extract

¾ teaspoon salt

⅔ teaspoon ground cinnamon

¼ teaspoon ground nutmeg

2 cups white bread flour

⅓ teaspoon bread machine or instant yeast

12 SLICES / 1 ½ POUNDS

¾ cup water, at 80°F to 90°F

1 egg, at room temperature

3 tablespoons butter, melted and cooled

3 tablespoons sugar

1 tablespoon rum extract

1¼ teaspoons salt

1 teaspoon ground cinnamon

¼ teaspoon ground nutmeg

3 cups white bread flour

1 teaspoon bread machine or instant yeast

16 SLICES / 2 POUNDS

1 cup plus 2 tablespoons water, at 80°F to 90°F

1 egg, at room temperature

¼ cup butter, melted and cooled

¼ cup sugar

4 teaspoons rum extract

1⅔ teaspoons salt

1⅓ teaspoons ground cinnamon

¼ teaspoon ground nutmeg

4 cups white bread flour

1⅓ teaspoons bread machine or instant yeast

1. Place the ingredients in your bread machine as recommended by the manufacturer.
2. Program the machine for Sweet bread and press Start.
3. When the loaf is done, remove the bucket from the machine.
4. Let the loaf cool for 5 minutes.
5. Gently shake the bucket to remove the loaf, and turn it out onto a rack to cool.

"Did You Know?" Hot buttered rum is a very popular beverage around the holidays and is often referred to as a hot toddy. This drink is meant to warm the body during bitterly cold winters, and the traditional preparation involved blending hot rum, water, and a buttered rum batter.

PER SERVING (1 SLICE): CALORIES: 161; TOTAL FAT: 4G; SATURATED FAT: 2G; CARBOHYDRATES: 27G; FIBER: 1G; SODIUM: 271MG; PROTEIN: 4G

—Chapter Eleven—

SWEET BREADS

Chocolate Chip Peanut Butter Banana Bread

PREP TIME IS 20 MINUTES OR LESS

Banana bread can be a healthy snack or dessert depending on what else is added to the batter. This version lands closer to the dessert side of the equation. The paddle action of the bread machine distributes the peanut butter chips quite evenly through the batter, so you will get to enjoy all the flavors in each bite.

12 TO 16 SLICES / 1 ½ TO 2 POUNDS

2 bananas, mashed

2 eggs, at room temperature

½ cup melted butter, cooled

2 tablespoons milk, at room temperature

1 teaspoon pure vanilla extract

2 cups all-purpose flour

½ cup sugar

1 ¼ teaspoons baking powder

½ teaspoon baking soda

½ teaspoon salt

½ cup peanut butter chips

½ cup semisweet chocolate chips

1. Stir together the bananas, eggs, butter, milk, and vanilla in the bread machine bucket and set it aside.
2. In a medium bowl, toss together the flour, sugar, baking powder, baking soda, salt, peanut butter chips, and chocolate chips.
3. Add the dry ingredients to the bucket.
4. Program the machine for Quick/Rapid bread, and press Start.
5. When the loaf is done, stick a knife into it, and if it comes out clean, the loaf is done.
6. If the loaf needs a few more minutes, check the control panel for a Bake Only button and extend the time by 10 minutes.
7. When the loaf is done, remove the bucket from the machine.
8. Let the loaf cool for 5 minutes.
9. Gently shake the bucket to remove the loaf, and turn it out onto a rack to cool.

Decoration tip: Try drizzling melted chocolate and melted peanut butter chips on the top of the cooled loaf. Your finished creation will be gorgeous and delicious!

PER SERVING (1 SLICE): CALORIES: 297; TOTAL FAT: 14G; SATURATED FAT: 7G; CARBOHYDRATES: 40G; FIBER: 1G; SODIUM: 255MG; PROTEIN: 4G

Chocolate Sour Cream Bread

PREP TIME IS 20 MINUTES OR LESS

Can you really make luscious, rich, brownie-like bread in your bread machine? The answer is a resounding "Yes!" Sour cream adds a tangy flavor and smooth texture to the loaf, which is complemented by sweet milk chocolate chips. Serve thick slices with a scoop of vanilla ice cream.

12 SLICES / 1 ½ TO 2 POUNDS

1 cup sour cream

2 eggs, at room temperature

1 cup sugar

½ cup (1 stick) butter, at room temperature

¼ cup plain Greek yogurt

1 ¾ cups all-purpose flour

½ cup unsweetened cocoa powder

½ teaspoon baking powder

½ teaspoon salt

1 cup milk chocolate chips

1. In a small bowl, whisk together the sour cream, eggs, sugar, butter, and yogurt until just combined.

2. Transfer the wet ingredients to the bread machine bucket, and then add the flour, cocoa powder, baking powder, salt, and chocolate chips.

3. Program the machine for Quick/Rapid bread, and press Start.

4. When the loaf is done, stick a knife into it, and if it comes out clean, the loaf is done.

5. If the loaf needs a few more minutes, check the control panel for a Bake Only button and extend the time by 10 minutes.

6. When the loaf is done, remove the bucket from the machine.

7. Let the loaf cool for 5 minutes.

8. Gently shake the bucket to remove the loaf, and turn it out onto a rack to cool.

Cooking tip: Try adding the wet ingredients and sugar to your bread machine and let the paddles do the creaming. When the ingredients are well mixed, add the dry ingredients and chips to the bucket.

PER SERVING (1 SLICE): CALORIES: 347; TOTAL FAT: 16G; SATURATED FAT: 9G; CARBOHYDRATES: 48G; FIBER: 2G; SODIUM: 249MG; PROTEIN: 6G

Nectarine Cobbler Bread

PREP TIME IS 10 MINUTES OR LESS

Cobbler is a dessert featuring a biscuit topping over any kind of fruit, including berries, plums, peaches, or any combination of mixed fruit. You can create an interesting crumbled top on this bread if you mix together oats, flour, brown sugar, butter, and a little cinnamon. Sprinkle the topping over the batter when the final mixing cycle is finished and let your bread machine do all the work.

12 TO 16 SLICES / 1 ½ TO 2 POUNDS

½ cup (1 stick) butter, at room temperature

2 eggs, at room temperature

1 cup sugar

¼ cup milk, at room temperature

1 teaspoon pure vanilla extract

1 cup diced nectarines

1 ¾ cups all-purpose flour

1 teaspoon baking soda

½ teaspoon salt

½ teaspoon ground nutmeg

¼ teaspoon baking powder

1. Place the butter, eggs, sugar, milk, vanilla, and nectarines in your bread machine.

2. Program the machine for Quick/Rapid bread and press Start.

3. While the wet ingredients are mixing, stir together the flour, baking soda, salt, nutmeg, and baking powder in a small bowl.

4. After the first fast mixing is done and the machine signals, add the dry ingredients.

5. When the loaf is done, remove the bucket from the machine.

6. Let the loaf cool for 5 minutes.

7. Gently shake the bucket to remove the loaf, and turn it out onto a rack to cool.

Decoration tip: If you are home during the baking cycle of this bread, you can decorate the top with thin slices of nectarine. When the final mixing cycle is finished, arrange the nectarine slices on the top of the batter in a pretty pattern or even rows.

PER SERVING (1 SLICE): CALORIES: 218; TOTAL FAT: 9G; SATURATED FAT: 5G; CARBOHYDRATES: 32G; FIBER: 1G; SODIUM: 270MG; PROTEIN: 3G

Sour Cream Maple Bread

PREP TIME IS 10 MINUTES OR LESS

Maple syrup offers a subtle sweetness to bread unlike the more assertive flavor of sugar or honey. You can serve slices of this bread as dessert because of its slightly cake-like texture, which comes from the addition of sour cream. Make sure the sour cream is full-fat rather than nonfat or low fat, so this recipe has the correct amount of fat to balance the sugar and yeast.

8 SLICES / 1 POUND	12 SLICES / 1½ POUNDS	16 SLICES / 2 POUNDS
6 tablespoons water, at 80°F to 90°F	½ cup plus 1 tablespoon water, at 80°F to 90°F	¾ cup water, at 80°F to 90°F
6 tablespoons sour cream, at room temperature	½ cup plus 1 tablespoon sour cream, at room temperature	¾ cup sour cream, at room temperature
1½ tablespoons butter, at room temperature	2¼ tablespoons butter, at room temperature	3 tablespoons butter, at room temperature
¾ tablespoon maple syrup	1 tablespoon maple syrup	1½ tablespoon maple syrup
½ teaspoon salt	¾ teaspoon salt	1 teaspoon salt
1¾ cups white bread flour	2¾ cups white bread flour	3¾ cups white bread flour
1⅛ teaspoons bread machine or instant yeast	1⅔ teaspoons bread machine or instant yeast	2¼ teaspoons bread machine or instant yeast

1. Place the ingredients in your bread machine as recommended by the manufacturer.
2. Program the machine for Basic/White bread, select light or medium crust, and press Start.
3. When the loaf is done, remove the bucket from the machine.
4. Let the loaf cool for 5 minutes.
5. Gently shake the bucket to remove the loaf, and turn it out onto a rack to cool.

Ingredient tip: Maple syrup comes in different grades depending on its strength and color. For this bread, look for the darkest maple syrup, which is Canada No. 3 dark or U.S. Grade C.

PER SERVING (1 SLICE): CALORIES: 149; TOTAL FAT: 4G; SATURATED FAT: 3G; CARBOHYDRATES: 24G; FIBER: 1G; SODIUM: 168MG; PROTEIN: 4G

Barmbrack Bread

PREP TIME IS 10 MINUTES OR LESS

Sweeter than regular bread but not quite dessert, this traditional Irish bread is perfect toasted and served with a cup of tea or coffee on a leisurely morning. Original recipes use raisins instead of currants and often omit the lemon zest. Experiment with the ingredients until you get the balance of flavor you enjoy.

8 SLICES / 1 POUND

⅔ cup water, at 80°F to 90°F

1 tablespoon melted butter, cooled

2 tablespoons sugar

2 tablespoons skim milk powder

1 teaspoon salt

1 teaspoon dried lemon zest

¼ teaspoon ground allspice

⅛ teaspoon ground nutmeg

2 cups white bread flour

1½ teaspoons bread machine or active dry yeast

½ cup dried currants

12 SLICES / 1½ POUNDS

1 cup plus 2 tablespoons water, at 80°F to 90°F

1½ tablespoons melted butter, cooled

3 tablespoons sugar

3 tablespoons skim milk powder

1½ teaspoons salt

1 teaspoon dried lemon zest

½ teaspoon ground allspice

¼ teaspoon ground nutmeg

3 cups white bread flour

2½ teaspoons bread machine or active dry yeast

¾ cup dried currants

16 SLICES / 2 POUNDS

1½ cups water, at 80°F to 90°F

2 tablespoons melted butter, cooled

¼ cup sugar

¼ cup skim milk powder

2 teaspoons salt

1½ teaspoons dried lemon zest

¾ teaspoon ground allspice

¼ teaspoon ground nutmeg

4 cups white bread flour

2½ teaspoons bread machine or active dry yeast

1 cup dried currants

1. Place the ingredients, except the currants, in your bread machine as recommended by the manufacturer.
2. Program the machine for Basic/White bread, select light or medium crust, and press Start.
3. Add the currants when your machine signals or when the second kneading cycle starts.
4. When the loaf is done, remove the bucket from the machine.
5. Let the loaf cool for 5 minutes.
6. Gently shake the bucket to remove the loaf, and turn it out onto a rack to cool.

Machine tip: If you use a nut and raisin hopper, toss the currants in a few tablespoons of flour (taken out of the flour measurement) to make sure they don't stick together and go into the bread smoothly.

PER SERVING (1 SLICE): CALORIES: 175; TOTAL FAT: 2G; SATURATED FAT: 1G; CARBOHYDRATES: 35G; FIBER: 1G; SODIUM: 313MG; PROTEIN: 5G

Apple Butter Bread

PREP TIME IS 10 MINUTES OR LESS

You will not have to add much sweetener to this recipe to create a well-risen loaf because the apple butter has plenty of sugar to feed the yeast adequately. The bread has a subtle apple taste, which is lovely spread with cream cheese or toasted topped with sharp Cheddar.

8 SLICES / 1 POUND	12 SLICES / 1½ POUNDS	16 SLICES / 2 POUNDS
⅔ cup milk, at 80°F to 90°F	1 cup milk, at 80°F to 90°F	1⅓ cups milk, at 80°F to 90°F
⅓ cup apple butter, at room temperature	½ cup apple butter, at room temperature	⅔ cup apple butter, at room temperature
4 teaspoons melted butter, cooled	2 tablespoons melted butter, cooled	2⅔ tablespoons melted butter, cooled
2 teaspoons honey	1 tablespoon honey	4 teaspoons honey
⅔ teaspoon salt	1 teaspoon salt	1⅓ teaspoons salt
⅔ cup whole-wheat flour	1 cup whole-wheat flour	1⅓ cups whole-wheat flour
1½ cups white bread flour	2¼ cups white bread flour	3 cups white bread flour
1 teaspoon bread machine or instant yeast	1½ teaspoons bread machine or instant yeast	2 teaspoons bread machine or instant yeast

1. Place the ingredients in your bread machine as recommended by the manufacturer.
2. Program the machine for Basic/White bread, select light or medium crust, and press Start.
3. When the loaf is done, remove the bucket from the machine.
4. Let the loaf cool for 5 minutes.
5. Gently shake the bucket to remove the loaf, and turn it out onto a rack to cool.

Ingredient tip: Apple butter is simple to make in a slow cooker with very little fuss or mess. Making your own ensures you know exactly what ingredients go into this tasty spread.

PER SERVING (1 SLICE): CALORIES: 178; TOTAL FAT: 3G; SATURATED FAT: 2G; CARBOHYDRATES: 34G; FIBER: 1G; SODIUM: 220MG; PROTEIN: 4G

Crusty Honey Bread

PREP TIME IS 10 MINUTES OR LESS

French bread traditionally contains no fat, so this cannot be considered real French-style bread, although it certainly tastes similar to a baguette. It has a crispy crust and tender crumb, with a little bit more sweetness from the honey. Spread a little butter on a slice warm from your bread machine and you might have a new family favorite.

8 SLICES / 1 POUND	12 SLICES / 1 ½ POUNDS	16 SLICES / 2 POUNDS
⅔ cup water, at 80°F to 90°F	1 cup minus 1 tablespoon water, at 80°F to 90°F	1 ¼ cups water, at 80°F to 90°F
1 tablespoon honey	1 ½ tablespoons honey	2 tablespoons honey
¾ tablespoon melted butter, cooled	1 ⅛ tablespoons melted butter, cooled	1 ½ tablespoons melted butter, cooled
½ teaspoon salt	¾ teaspoon salt	1 teaspoon salt
1 ¾ cups white bread flour	2 ⅔ cups white bread flour	3 ½ cups white bread flour
1 teaspoon bread machine or instant yeast	1 ½ teaspoons bread machine or instant yeast	2 teaspoons bread machine or instant yeast

1. Place the ingredients in your bread machine as recommended by the manufacturer.
2. Program the machine for Basic/White bread, select light or medium crust, and press Start.
3. When the loaf is done, remove the bucket from the machine.
4. Let the loaf cool for 5 minutes.
5. Gently shake the bucket to remove the loaf, and turn it out onto a rack to cool.

Variation tip: Try adding semisweet chocolate chips and/or butterscotch chips for an unexpected twist on this simple bread. The resulting product will be gilded with sweetness that gives the plain version a major face-lift.

PER SERVING (1 SLICE): CALORIES: 119; TOTAL FAT: 1G; SATURATED FAT: 1G; CARBOHYDRATES: 24G; FIBER: 1G; SODIUM: 155MG; PROTEIN: 3G

Honey Granola Bread

PREP TIME IS 10 MINUTES OR LESS

Homemade granola would be spectacular in this loaf because you can control exactly which oil and sweeteners are in it. Heavily sweetened granola would provide too much sugar for the yeast in the recipe, and your bread might rise too high. Look for prepared granola with only a touch of honey or cane sugar for the best results.

8 SLICES / 1 POUND	12 SLICES / 1½ POUNDS	16 SLICES / 2 POUNDS
¾ cups milk, at 80°F to 90°F	1⅛ cups milk, at 80°F to 90°F	1½ cups milk, at 80°F to 90°F
2 tablespoons honey	3 tablespoons honey	¼ cup honey
1 tablespoon butter, melted and cooled	1½ tablespoons butter, melted and cooled	2 tablespoons butter, melted and cooled
¾ teaspoons salt	1⅛ teaspoons salt	1½ teaspoons salt
½ cup whole-wheat flour	¾ cup whole-wheat flour	1 cup whole-wheat flour
½ cup prepared granola, crushed	⅔ cup prepared granola, crushed	¾ cup prepared granola, crushed
1¼ cups white bread flour	1¾ cups white bread flour	2½ cups white bread flour
1 teaspoon bread machine or instant yeast	1½ teaspoons bread machine or instant yeast	2 teaspoons bread machine or instant yeast

1. Place the ingredients in your bread machine as recommended by the manufacturer.
2. Program the machine for Basic/White bread, select light or medium crust, and press Start.
3. When the loaf is done, remove the bucket from the machine.
4. Let the loaf cool for 5 minutes.
5. Gently shake the bucket to remove the loaf, and turn it out onto a rack to cool.

Ingredient tip: Choose a granola with no dried fruit in it, because you will be crushing it for this recipe. Dried fruit would create a lumpy mess in the dough, which would wreck the texture of the finished loaf.

PER SERVING (1 SLICE): CALORIES: 151; TOTAL FAT: 5G; SATURATED FAT: 2G; CARBOHYDRATES: 33G; FIBER: 2G; SODIUM: 218MG; PROTEIN: 6G

Black Bread

PREP TIME IS 10 MINUTES OR LESS

Cocoa powder, rye flour, molasses, and coffee create the signature look and flavor of this finished loaf. Blackstrap molasses would also be a nice choice to intensify the already distinctive taste. You might be surprised by the hint of sweetness in this bread.

8 SLICES / 1 POUND

½ cup water, at 80°F to 90°F

¼ cup brewed coffee, at 80°F to 90°F

1 tablespoon balsamic vinegar

1 tablespoon olive oil

1 tablespoon dark molasses

½ tablespoon light brown sugar

½ teaspoon salt

1 teaspoon caraway seeds

2 tablespoons unsweetened cocoa powder

½ cup dark rye flour

1¼ cups white bread flour

1 teaspoon bread machine or instant yeast

12 SLICES / 1½ POUNDS

¾ cup water, at 80°F to 90°F

⅓ cup brewed coffee, at 80°F to 90°F

1½ tablespoons balsamic vinegar

1½ tablespoons olive oil

1½ tablespoons dark molasses

¾ tablespoon light brown sugar

¾ teaspoon salt

1½ teaspoons caraway seeds

3 tablespoons unsweetened cocoa powder

¾ cup dark rye flour

1¾ cups white bread flour

1½ teaspoons bread machine or instant yeast

16 SLICES / 2 POUNDS

1 cup water, at 80°F to 90°F

½ cup brewed coffee, at 80°F to 90°F

2 tablespoons balsamic vinegar

2 tablespoons olive oil

2 tablespoons dark molasses

1 tablespoon light brown sugar

1 teaspoon salt

2 teaspoons caraway seeds

¼ cup unsweetened cocoa powder

1 cup dark rye flour

2½ cups white bread flour

2 teaspoons bread machine or instant yeast

→

1. Place the ingredients in your bread machine as recommended by the manufacturer.
2. Program the machine for Whole-Wheat/Whole-Grain bread, select light or medium crust, and press Start.
3. When the loaf is done, remove the bucket from the machine.
4. Let the loaf cool for 5 minutes.
5. Gently shake the bucket to remove the loaf, and turn it out onto a rack to cool.

"Did You Know?" Black bread is a staple in Russian cuisine and frequently seen as a symbol of health and prosperity. It is also sometimes tied to the history of hardships in the country when it was a main food source during times when other food wasn't readily available. Traditional recipes for black bread are known for their richness and complexity, and can be quite involved to make from scratch.

PER SERVING (1 SLICE): CALORIES: 123; TOTAL FAT: 2G; SATURATED FAT: 0G; CARBOHYDRATES: 23G; FIBER: 3G; SODIUM: 150MG; PROTEIN: 4G

Apple Cider Bread

PREP TIME IS 10 MINUTES OR LESS

Warm mugs of steaming cider held between mitten-covered hands are a good memory for many people who grew up in cold climates. The spices and hint of cider in this apple-studded bread make it something exceptional. The best way to serve this bread is warmed and smeared with butter.

8 SLICES / 1 POUND	12 SLICES / 1½ POUNDS	16 SLICES / 2 POUNDS
¼ cup milk, at 80°F to 90°F	5 tablespoons milk, at 80°F to 90°F	½ cup minus 1 tablespoon milk, at 80°F to 90°F
2 tablespoons apple cider, at room temperature	3 tablespoons apple cider, at room temperature	¼ cup apple cider, at room temperature
2 tablespoons sugar	3 tablespoons sugar	¼ cup sugar
4 teaspoons melted butter, cooled	2 tablespoons melted butter, cooled	2⅔ tablespoons melted butter, cooled
1 tablespoon honey	1½ tablespoons honey	2 tablespoons honey
¼ teaspoon salt	¼ teaspoon salt	¼ teaspoon salt
2 cups white bread flour	3 cups white bread flour	4 cups white bread flour
¾ teaspoons bread machine or instant yeast	1¼ teaspoons bread machine or instant yeast	1⅔ teaspoons bread machine or instant yeast
⅔ apple, peeled, cored, and finely diced	1 apple, peeled, cored, and finely diced	1 apple, peeled, cored, and finely diced

1. Place the ingredients, except the apple, in your bread machine as recommended by the manufacturer.
2. Program the machine for Basic/White bread, select light or medium crust, and press Start.
3. Add the apple when the machine signals or 5 minutes before the last kneading cycle is complete.
4. When the loaf is done, remove the bucket from the machine.
5. Let the loaf cool for 5 minutes.
6. Gently shake the bucket to remove the loaf, and turn it out onto a rack to cool.

Ingredient tip: Look for apple cider that is sweetened and spiced well so your bread rises nicely.

PER SERVING (1 SLICE): CALORIES: 164; TOTAL FAT: 3G; SATURATED FAT: 1G;CARBOHYDRATES: 31G; FIBER: 1G; SODIUM: 70MG; PROTEIN: 4G

Coffee Cake

PREP TIME IS 10 MINUTES OR LESS

This loaf is both a coffee cake and bread made with coffee. Instant coffee granules impart a decisive coffee flavor to the bread, and a slice will be perfect for breakfast or as part of a brunch spread. Sprinkle some powdered sugar on top, cut into slices, and enjoy!

12 TO 16 SLICES / 1½ TO 2 POUNDS

¾ cup buttermilk, at room temperature

¾ cup (1½ sticks) butter, at room temperature

1 tablespoon instant coffee granules

3 eggs, at room temperature

¾ cup sugar

2 cups all-purpose flour

½ tablespoon baking powder

½ teaspoon salt

1 cup chopped pecans

1. Place the buttermilk, butter, coffee granules, eggs, and sugar in your bread machine.
2. Program the machine for Quick/Rapid bread and press Start.
3. While the wet ingredients are mixing, stir together the flour, baking powder, salt, and pecans in a small bowl.
4. After the first fast mixing is done and the machine signals, add the dry ingredients.
5. When the loaf is done, remove the bucket from the machine.
6. Let the loaf cool for 5 minutes.
7. Gently shake the bucket to remove the loaf, and turn it out onto a rack to cool.

Variation tip: You can use walnuts, macadamia nuts, or even chopped almonds in this recipe. Try a different type of nut each time you make this coffee cake.

PER SERVING (1 SLICE): CALORIES: 273; TOTAL FAT: 15G; SATURATED FAT: 8G; CARBOHYDRATES: 30G; FIBER: 1G; SODIUM: 213MG; PROTEIN: 5G

Pumpkin Coconut Bread

PREP TIME IS 10 MINUTES OR LESS

This bread can be described as moist, pleasantly spiced, and perfect for breakfast or as an afternoon snack. Pumpkin and coconut have a natural flavor affinity, combining earthy with sweet and nutty. Make sure you use pure canned pumpkin rather than pumpkin pie filling, which has added sugar and other ingredients.

12 TO 16 SLICES / 1 ½ TO 2 POUNDS

1 cup pure canned pumpkin

½ cup (1 stick) butter, at room temperature

1 ½ teaspoons pure vanilla extract

1 cup sugar

½ cup dark brown sugar

2 cups all-purpose flour

¾ cup sweetened shredded coconut

1 ½ teaspoons ground cinnamon

1 teaspoon baking soda

1 teaspoon baking powder

½ teaspoon ground nutmeg

½ teaspoon ground ginger

⅛ teaspoon ground allspice

1. Place the pumpkin, butter, vanilla, sugar, and dark brown sugar in your bread machine.
2. Program the machine for Quick/Rapid bread and press Start.
3. After the first fast mixing is done, add the flour, coconut, cinnamon, baking soda, baking powder, nutmeg, ginger, and allspice.
4. When the loaf is done, remove the bucket from the machine.
5. Let the loaf cool for 5 minutes.
6. Gently shake the bucket to remove the loaf, and turn it out onto a rack to cool.

"Did You Know?" Pumpkin truly is a "superfood," and there's no need to choose fresh pumpkin to get the health benefits. One cup of canned pumpkin has 7 grams of fiber and 3 grams of protein—even more than in fresh pumpkin—and contains only 80 calories and 1 gram of fat. Plus, it is packed with antioxidants and disease-fighting vitamins.

PER SERVING (1 SLICE): CALORIES: 269; TOTAL FAT: 11G; SATURATED FAT: 6G; CARBOHYDRATES: 42G; FIBER: 2G; SODIUM: 171MG; PROTEIN: 4G

Vanilla Almond Milk Bread

PREP TIME IS 10 MINUTES OR LESS

The aroma that will waft from this bread machine during the baking cycle will draw anyone in the house to the kitchen in anticipation. Sweet vanilla and a hint of almond infuse this golden loaf with enough flavor to entice without being overwhelming. You can use vanilla extract if you don't have almond extract handy.

8 SLICES / 1 POUND

⅓ cup plus 1 tablespoon milk, at 80°F to 90°F

2 tablespoons melted butter, cooled

2 tablespoons sugar

1 egg, at room temperature

1 teaspoon pure vanilla extract

¼ teaspoon pure almond extract

1⅔ cups white bread flour

1 teaspoon bread machine or instant yeast

12 SLICES / 1½ POUNDS

½ cup plus 1 tablespoon milk, at 80°F to 90°F

3 tablespoons melted butter, cooled

3 tablespoons sugar

1 egg, at room temperature

1½ teaspoons pure vanilla extract

⅓ teaspoon almond extract

2½ cups white bread flour

1½ teaspoons bread machine or instant yeast

16 SLICES / 2 POUNDS

¾ cup milk, at 80°F to 90°F

¼ cup melted butter, cooled

¼ cup sugar

1 egg, at room temperature

2 teaspoons pure vanilla extract

½ teaspoon almond extract

3⅓ cups white bread flour

2 teaspoons bread machine or instant yeast

1. Place the ingredients in your bread machine as recommended by the manufacturer.
2. Program the machine for Basic/White bread, select light or medium crust, and press Start.
3. When the loaf is done, remove the bucket from the machine.
4. Let the loaf cool for 5 minutes.
5. Gently shake the bucket to remove the loaf, and turn it out onto a rack to cool.

Variation tip: Add the seeds from an entire vanilla bean to your 2-pound loaf with the wet ingredients instead of the extract for a more intense flavor. Use one-half bean for the 1-pound loaf and three-fourths of a bean for the 1½-pound loaf.

PER SERVING (1 SLICE): CALORIES: 146; TOTAL FAT: 4G; SATURATED FAT: 2G; CARBOHYDRATES: 24G; FIBER: 1G; SODIUM: 33MG; PROTEIN: 4G

Triple Chocolate Bread

PREP TIME IS 10 MINUTES OR LESS

Unlike quick breads, which have a cake texture, this is a true yeast-raised bread studded with both dark and white chocolate chips. You probably won't want to toast it, but it is delicious when used to make French toast. The white chocolate chips seem to get a caramel taste when they brown up on the crust side.

8 SLICES / 1 POUND

⅔ cup milk, at 80°F to 90°F

1 egg, at room temperature

1½ tablespoons melted butter, cooled

1 teaspoon pure vanilla extract

2 tablespoons light brown sugar

1 tablespoon unsweetened cocoa powder

½ teaspoon salt

2 cups white bread flour

1 teaspoon bread machine or instant yeast

¼ cup semisweet chocolate chips

¼ cup white chocolate chips

12 SLICES / 1½ POUNDS

1 cup milk, at 80°F to 90°F

1 egg, at room temperature

2 tablespoons melted butter, cooled

1½ teaspoons pure vanilla extract

3 tablespoons light brown sugar

4 teaspoons unsweetened cocoa powder

¾ teaspoon salt

3 cups white bread flour

1¼ teaspoons bread machine or instant yeast

⅓ cup semisweet chocolate chips

⅓ cup white chocolate chips

16 SLICES / 2 POUNDS

1⅓ cup milk, at 80°F to 90°F

1 egg, at room temperature

2⅔ tablespoons melted butter, cooled

2 teaspoons pure vanilla extract

¼ cup light brown sugar

2 tablespoons unsweetened cocoa powder

1 teaspoon salt

4 cups white bread flour

1⅔ teaspoons bread machine or instant yeast

½ cup semisweet chocolate chips

½ cup white chocolate chips

→

1. Place the ingredients, except the chocolate chips, in your bread machine as recommended by the manufacturer.

2. Program the machine for Basic/White bread, select light or medium crust, and press Start.

3. When the machine signals, add the chocolate chips, or put them in the nut/raisin hopper and the machine will add them automatically.

4. When the loaf is done, remove the bucket from the machine.

5. Let the loaf cool for 5 minutes.

6. Gently shake the bucket to remove the loaf, and turn it out onto a rack to cool.

Variation tip: Chopped hazelnuts, pecans, or peanuts will add a welcome crunch to the bread. Substitute the nuts for either the white or semisweet chocolate chips so your bread is not too packed with ingredients.

PER SERVING (1 SLICE): CALORIES: 230; TOTAL FAT: 7G; SATURATED FAT: 4G; CARBOHYDRATES: 36G; FIBER: 1G; SODIUM: 207MG; PROTEIN: 5G

Chocolate Oatmeal Banana Bread

PREP TIME IS 10 MINUTES OR LESS

In addition to having a perfectly sweet chocolate flavor, this bread is a great use for the bananas sitting on your counter. The oats are a healthy addition that give it great texture and make it hearty. Simply set the machine and enjoy a loaf with no fuss or mess.

12 TO 16 SLICES / 1 ½ TO 2 POUNDS

3 bananas, mashed

2 eggs, at room temperature

¾ cup packed light brown sugar

½ cup (1 stick) butter, at room temperature

½ cup sour cream, at room temperature

¼ cup sugar

1 ½ teaspoons pure vanilla extract

1 cup all-purpose flour

½ cup quick oats

2 tablespoons unsweetened cocoa powder

1 teaspoon baking soda

1. Place the banana, eggs, brown sugar, butter, sour cream, sugar, and vanilla in your bread machine.

2. Program the machine for Quick/Rapid bread and press Start.

3. While the wet ingredients are mixing, stir together the flour, oats, cocoa powder, and baking soda in a small bowl.

4. After the first fast mixing is done and the machine signals, add the dry ingredients.

5. When the loaf is done, remove the bucket from the machine.

6. Let the loaf cool for 5 minutes.

7. Gently shake the bucket to remove the loaf, and turn it out onto a rack to cool.

Variation tip: Mini chocolate chips, peanut butter chips, chopped pecans, or white chocolate chips would all create delicious variations of this dessert–like bread. Add about ½ cup to ¾ cup to the batter after the first fast mixing cycle.

PER SERVING (1 SLICE): CALORIES: 231; TOTAL FAT: 11G; SATURATED FAT: 6G; CARBOHYDRATES: 31G; FIBER: 2G; SODIUM: 179MG; PROTEIN: 4G

APPENDIX
CONVERSION TABLES

Volume Equivalents (Liquid)

US STANDARD	US STANDARD (OUNCES)	METRIC (APPROXIMATE)
2 tablespoons	1 fl. oz.	30 mL
¼ cup	2 fl. oz.	60 mL
½ cup	4 fl. oz.	120 mL
1 cup	8 fl. oz.	240 mL
1½ cups	12 fl. oz.	355 mL
2 cups or 1 pint	16 fl. oz.	475 mL
4 cups or 1 quart	32 fl. oz.	1 L
1 gallon	128 fl. oz.	4 L

Oven Temperatures

FAHRENHEIT (°F)	CELSIUS (°C) (APPROXIMATE)
250°F	120°C
300°F	150°C
325°F	165°C
350°F	180°C
375°F	190°C
400°F	200°C
425°F	220°C
450°F	230°C

Volume Equivalents (Dry)

US STANDARD	METRIC (APPROXIMATE)
⅛ teaspoon	0.5 mL
¼ teaspoon	1 mL
½ teaspoon	2 mL
¾ teaspoon	4 mL
1 teaspoon	5 mL
1 tablespoon	15 mL
¼ cup	59 mL
⅓ cup	79 mL
½ cup	118 mL
⅔ cup	156 mL
¾ cup	177 mL
1 cup	235 mL
2 cups or 1 pint	475 mL
3 cups	700 mL
4 cups or 1 quart	1 L
½ gallon	2 L
1 gallon	4 L

Weight Equivalents

US STANDARD	METRIC (APPROXIMATE)
½ ounce	15 g
1 ounce	30 g
2 ounces	60 g
4 ounces	115 g
8 ounces	225 g
12 ounces	340 g
16 ounces or 1 pound	455 g

RECIPE INDEX

INDEX

NOTES

NOTES

NOTES

NOTES

NOTES